THE YEARS OF TALKING
DANGEROUSLY

THE YEARS OF TALKING
DANGEROUSLY

GEOFFREY NUNBERG

PUBLICAFFAIRS
NEW YORK

Copyright © 2009 by Geoffrey Nunberg

Published in the United States by PublicAffairs™, a member of the Perseus
Books Group.

PublicAffairs books are available at special discounts for bulk purchases in the U.S.
by corporations, institutions, and other organizations. For more information,
please contact the Special Markets Department at the Perseus Books Group, 2300
Chestnut Street, Suite 200, Philadelphia, PA 19103, call (800) 810-4145, ext. 5000,
or e-mail special.markets@perseusbooks.com.

Designed by Jeff Williams
Text set in 12-point Dante MT

Library of Congress Cataloging-in-Publication Data

Nunberg, Geoffrey, 1945–
    The years of talking dangerously / Geoffrey Nunberg.
        p. cm.
    Includes index.
    ISBN 978-1-58648-745-4 (alk. paper)
    1. English language—Political aspects—United States. 2. English language—
Social aspects—United States. 3. English language—United States—Semantics.
4. English language—United States—Usage. 5. United States—Politics and
government—2001– I. Title.
    PE2809.N875 2009
    306.440973—dc22

                                                              2009000249

First Edition
10 9 8 7 6 5 4 3 2 1

CONTENTS

ENGLISH 2.0

SYMBOLS

INTRODUCTION

The pieces collected here are snapshots of the language during the final years of the Bush era. Of course labeling a stretch of time as an "era" tends to make it seem tidier and more coherent than it actually was. *Islamo-fascism* and *intrapreneur, ownership* and *under the bus, marriage* and *macaca*—what exactly do they have in common, other than that they were all airing in the same season? You think of a TV commercial for one of those *Hits of the 1970s* compilation CDs, with a montage of images of beanbag chairs, the fall of Saigon, streakers, Kent State, Bruce Lee, and *Saturday Night Fever* flashing across the screen against a soundtrack by Gloria Gaynor, Kenny Rogers, and The Clash.

That sense of disconnected jumble is inescapable when you try to pin down "the state of the language." At any given time there are a lot of different things going on that leave their marks on the way we speak, each moshing to its own rhythm. There are changes in technology, which have not only added perky new words like *blogosphere, splog,* and *twitter* (a clear improvement on older, clunkier neologisms formed with prefixes like *virtual* and *cyber*) but pioneered new frontiers in English orthography, a glimpse of the way we'll all write when the st8 hz withrd awA. (See "All Thumbs.") There are the subtle shifts in sensibility that would be hard to pin down if the language didn't give them away. *Snarky* was doing quiet duty as British slang for "ill-tempered" until a decade or so ago, when journalists and bloggers repurposed it as a vogue word for the territory between bitchy and cheeky. Whatever exactly precipitated the shift, it was the same spirit that led people to start using *um* to introduce sarcastic corrections of other people's foolish mistakes, as in "Um . . . you might try plugging it in first" ("Pause for Thought").

Some innovations seem to answer only to the caprices of fashion. I can come up with a story about why *throw so-and-so under the bus* suddenly caught on to describe a self-serving betrayal ("Under the Bus"). But I suspect it has the after-the-fact feel of most explanations of fads and vogues. (In retrospect, it seems historically inevitable that the 1970s should have seen the rise of the four-inch platform shoe, but it would probably have seemed just as inevitable if the decade had wound up shuffling around in flats.)

Then there are the evanescent items that linger for only as long as the news stories they were connected to. *Macaca* made its first and only appearance in the language in 2006, when Senator George Allen used it to refer to an Indian American at a campaign rally; the ensuing ruckus probably cost Allen a close election and tipped the Senate to the Democrats. The public's interest in *persistent vegetative state* expired with Terri Schiavo. And *dwarf planet* swam into our ken for a month or so that same year when astronomers voted to strip Pluto of its full planetary citizenship ("Last Planet Standing").

The Pluto affair showed how purely semantic squabbles could penetrate even the austere reaches of the hard sciences. In the end, of course, it makes no difference to astronomy whether Pluto is classified as a planet or a "trans-Neptunian object," though apparently it mattered quite a bit to astronomers. And the planet's demotion was embarrassingly ad hoc, since the new definition of a planet is to apply only to objects in our own solar system (you could think of it as an example of what legal scholars call "result-oriented jurisprudence," like the Supreme Court's decision in *Bush v. Gore*). But then, as the *New York Times'* Clyde Haberman pointed out, most redefinitions are made for the sake of convenience, not to change anything in the world. The New York City Transit Authority's adoption of a more elastic definition of *on time* didn't change how long subway riders had to wait on the platform. The New York Knicks' redefinition of *sellout* didn't make the empty seats in Madison Square Garden any less visible. It's all semantics—along with *label* and *rhetoric*, a word that naturally attracts dismissive modifiers like *just* and *mere* ("A Duck by Any Other Name").

But that dismissal of "mere semantics" sits uneasily with the importance that people attach to names and labels and the lengths they'll go to in bending definitions to their purposes. Take the administration's reaction to charges of prisoner abuse at Guantanamo and elsewhere. Americans don't torture, the president insisted indignantly, but the Justice Department was obliged to qualify the assertion with an intricately argued footnote explicating the fine distinction between out-and-out torture and what Bush and Cheney described as "enhanced interrogation techniques" ("The Language of Abuse"). It was an uncharacteristically crude Orwellism for an administration that usually managed language more deftly. That tin ear was also evident when the White House press secretary Tony Snow proposed *sectarian violence aimed at expressing differences* as an alternative to *civil war* to describe the Sunni-Shia conflict in Iraq.

The fact is that it's impossible to talk about social or political values without wading knee-deep into questions about what ought to count as what. It's hard to think of an important recent story or controversy that hasn't forced us to reexamine the meanings of familiar words that we used to take for granted.

Sometimes the ethical issues surrounding a story are crystallized in an incidental semantic dilemma. Looking at the images from Katrina, we were forced to confront the subtleties of *looting*: was it right to use the same verb for carrying off a flat-screen TV from a Best Buy and taking diapers from a convenience store, particularly when the authorities had made such a mess of the relief efforts ("When Words Break Down")? And sometimes our views on an issue are inextricably connected to what we decide to call things. In surveys, people are a lot more likely to support laws that allow doctors to help "end the lives" of terminally ill patients who request it than to "help them commit suicide." Opponents of the laws criticize phrases like *aid in dying* as deceptive euphemisms, but supporters argue that *suicide* isn't really appropriate in this case, pointing out that the media and authorities avoided using the word for the people who jumped from the World Trade Center ("The Language of Death"). The debate may be semantic, but it's anything but "mere"—until you've decided what to call things, you don't know where they fit in the moral scheme of the universe.

But when I chose the title of this book, I wasn't thinking of the way people talked about planets, blogs, or even suicide. Prediction is a mug's game, but my guess is that when people look back on the language of the early years of the twenty-first century, the first thing that will come to mind is the political vocabulary—well, that and the language of real estate—just as the sixties evoke the language of rock, drugs, and disaffection; the seventies evoke the language of disco and New Age; the eighties evoke management jargon and Valley Girl slang; and the nineties evoke techno-talk and fit-speak. That's partly because the era has been more rancorously political than any period since the sixties, but it's also because people have given so much attention to political language itself.

At the outset, the Bush administration and its allies seemed to conduct symbolic politics more adroitly than anyone since the early years of the New Deal. They didn't simply package their messages succinctly and memorably; they coordinated the language of all the quarters of the right, from the think tanks to Congress to the radio and cable talk shows, and managed to cajole or intimidate much of the media into going along. The efforts seemed to be so successful that by the 2004 election, the Republicans' dominance of the political discourse had become something of an idée fixe among the Democrats, many of whom blamed the party's electoral eclipse on its problems with framing, messaging, and branding. How could the Republicans persuade so many voters to ignore their own best interests, if not by handing them a snappy line of patter?

But our faith in the power of words can be overdone. Not that language doesn't cast a long shadow on truth, as Auden put it—embellishing, disguising, palliating, making things sound grander or baser than they really are. But language can't keep reality at a distance indefinitely: when the dissonance becomes too great, something has to give. And by the end of the Bush presidency, the administration's language lay in tatters, emblematic of its substantive failures. Bush himself conceded as much in an interview just after the 2008 election, when he said he regretted having said things like "wanted dead or alive" and "bring 'em on" and appearing beneath the "Mission Accomplished" banner on the USS *Abraham Lincoln* in May 2003. "I was trying to convey a message," Bush said. "I could have conveyed it more artfully."

But it wasn't artlessness that undid the language; it was the stubborn disparity between words and things. By the 2006 midterm elections, as the public was losing patience with the Iraq war, the administration was already issuing slogan recalls. "We've never been stay the course," Bush told George Stephanopoulos just before the election, as if he could unsay hundreds of repetitions of the phrase. The White House floated *Islamo-fascism* around the same time in an effort to equate the war on terror to the last great war against absolute evil, but no one but neoconservatives found the analogy compelling, and within a few months the phrase had disappeared from Bush's and Cheney's speeches (*"Islamo-Creeps* Would Be More Accurate"). The language of the administration's domestic policy fared no better: *the ownership society* was quietly dropped after failure of the administration's Social Security privatization plan, and *Clear Skies* was dropped even earlier ("Even in English It's Hard to Translate").

Of course those catchphrases were bound to lose their power sooner or later. Once a euphemism becomes threadbare, either it's abandoned, like most of the Bush-era slogans, or it loses its euphemistic character and becomes a neutral name. *Recession, welfare,* and *affirmative action* began their lives as euphemisms, and *Social Security* was disparaged as a "glittering title" when the program was first proposed in 1936. Or consider the recent fortunes of *home equity loan*. Banks introduced the term in the early 1980s as a consumer-friendly name for second mortgages, which were associated with finance companies who preyed on homeowners desperate for funds. But the connotations of prudent husbandry that *home equity loan* was supposed to evoke were quickly forgotten once the proportions of the mortgage crisis became evident in 2007.

By the end of the Bush era, though, one could sense a sea change more significant than the eclipse of a few catchphrases. The 2008 election demonstrated the enervation of the language with which the right had been prosecuting the culture wars since the Nixon years. Not that the Republicans weren't still trying. *Country first, palling around with terrorists, raising the white flag of surrender, the pro-America areas of this great nation,* and finally, a little desperately, *socialist*—no campaign in recent memory has worked the language of patriotism and cultural populism as energetically and, in the end, as fruitlessly, as McCain and Palin did. Not even the combined efforts of Joe the Plumber and the Joe Sixpack–identified vice presidential candidate could stanch the defections from the middle-American voters that Republicans had been tenaciously cultivating since the Nixon era ("Just a Thing Called Joe," "The Ism Dismalest of All").

Of course you could argue that economic issues simply trumped cultural ones in this election or that these Republican candidates weren't the right messengers for charging Obama with being unpatriotic and subversive: Republicans suspected that McCain didn't really believe that charge, and everybody else was scared that Palin really did. But whatever happens in the next few years, it's hard to imagine the Republicans riding back into Pennsylvania and Ohio with the same bumper stickers the next time around. Their language suffers from a kind of structure fatigue, brought on by the strain of spanning the increasing distance between its literal and symbolic meanings.

Take the epithet *elite*, which worked so well for cultural populists in the past, precisely because it managed to marry its original sense of power and wealth with implications of upper-crust snootiness (that's what made John Kerry so vulnerable to the charge). Once the word becomes simply a marker of attitude—once its members are defined, as Laura Ingraham says, "not so much by class or wealth or position as they are by a *general outlook"*—then it becomes just another way of calling somebody stuck up. You could hear that shift at the moment in the campaign when Lady Lynn Forester de Rothschild, an American multimillionaire who married an heir to the Rothschild banking fortune, announced on CNN that she was switching her support from Hillary Clinton to John McCain and charged that Barack Obama couldn't connect with ordinary Americans because he was an elitist—and that so, by the way, was Wolf Blitzer. The remark was greeted with the derision it merited (she should ask her husband to explain to her the concept of chutzpah), but she really wasn't taking any more liberties with the word than upper-middle-class Ivy Leaguers like Ingraham and Ann Coulter, who are only a foreign preposition and a zero or two short of de Rothschild's station. Indeed, you get a sense of how condescending this ostensibly "classless" use of *elite* is when you realize that practically the only people who use the word that way are the ones who would qualify as elite in its traditional sense ("Where the Elites Meet").

That isn't to say the right is about to retire the vocabulary of populism. Some of it will hang around for a long time in the form of what linguists call a hearth language, the stage a dying language passes through when it is used only by familiars around the kitchen table (or what passes for the kitchen table in the age of blogs). But the language can be effective for Republicans only if it's reinvigorated with some genuine economic content. McCain and Palin acknowledged as much toward the end of the 2008 campaign with their attacks on "predatory lenders" and "greed and corruption on Wall Street." But as the Bush administration learned with *ownership society* and the rest, voters won't respond to that language unless they perceive that the Republicans have a second shoe to drop.

But as it happens the Democrats are facing something of the same linguistic challenge, even if it's a little less urgent. The striking thing about the collapse of the language of the right is that it was achieved without the Democrats making any real effort to neutralize it or replace it with some new language of their own. The Obama campaign made the perfunctory noises about patriotism, but there was nothing like the effort to co-opt the right's language that the Democratic campaign had made in 2004, which was launched with Kerry's "reporting for duty" and billed itself "a celebration of American values." That was probably wise—words like *values* and *traditional* can't simply be shorn of forty years of accumulated associations to be appropriated for the other side. And Obama did just fine confining himself to soaring evocations of hope and change. But while that has obviously been effective for him, you didn't hear the stirrings of any new tunes that other Democrats could sing along with. The strength of the right's language of cultural populism, after all, is that it could be effective even for singularly uncharismatic figures like John Kyl and Mitch McConnell.

It will take a while for the new languages of left and right to emerge—from very early on, it's looking like the candidates for 2009's word of the year will be something down-to-earth like *shovel-ready* or *workout* (of your mortgage, I mean, not of your abs). It's hard to imagine what the language of politics will sound like a decade from now, on both sides. But it's a good bet it will change more in that period than it has in the last quarter century. It won't be long before the language of the last few years sounds very retro indeed.

One lesson of these exercises is that there's no place you can't get to when you take language as your starting point—which is to say that you're almost sure to wind up in unfamiliar territory. So I'm thankful to all the guides I could turn to for help, particularly Leo Braudy, Rachel Brownstein, Paul Duguid, Kathleen Miller, Barbara Nunberg, Scott Parker, Tom Wasow, my co-bloggers at Language Log, and especially Bob Newsom.

I'm grateful as always to Phyllis Myers, the *Fresh Air* producer who has worked with me companionably and patiently over the years, almost always under a deadline I've cut too close, and to Terry Gross, Danny Miller, and the others who created and sustained the program that I have been fortunate to be associated with since it was launched more than twenty years ago. (Hitch your wagon to a star, people tell you, but really, who knew?) Thanks, too, to my agent, Joe Spieler, and to Clive Priddle, my editor at PublicAffairs. And thanks, once more, to Sophie Nunberg, who has progressed over the years from being a source of material to being a source of advice.

These pieces appear here pretty much as they did on the radio or in the press, though I've taken the opportunity to make some edits, correct a few factual errors, and include material that had to be cut in the original versions (or on a couple of occasions, bleeped—rest assured that I didn't say *those* words on the radio). In pieces that appeared in the *New York Times*, I've also eliminated some peculiarities of *Times*-style, like the insistent use of "Mr." and "Ms."; it seemed odd to refer to the president as "Mr. Bush" on one page and simply as "Bush" on another. And with pieces that originally appeared in the press, I've occasionally restored my original title when I felt the title it was given by the editors was uninspired. But I resisted the temptation to revise pieces to make me look more prescient in retrospect.

WATCHING OUR WORDS

BY HEART

Fresh Air Commentary, June 20, 2005

A few years ago, Ruth Lilly, the heir to a pharmaceutical fortune, left a $100 million bequest to *Poetry* magazine. Armed with what have to be the deepest coffers of any literary publication in history, the foundation established by the magazine's publishers recently joined with the National Endowment for the Arts to hold the first of a series of recitation competitions patterned after the national Spelling Bee.

I have to say I'm a little uneasy about that model. The national Spelling Bee is one of those odd competitions that turn an ordinary activity into a high-performance event, like extreme ironing. And when you think of poetry recitation contests, you might have the image of overachiever kids declaiming "The Boy Stood on the Burning Deck" with appropriate gestures, while their parents and elocution coaches watch nervously from the audience.

But that's probably unfair. You have to welcome any program that might encourage more learning of poetry by heart, after a half century you could think of as the Great Forgetting.

"In Xanadu did Kubla Khan . . . "; "I wandered lonely as a cloud"; "The Assyrian came down like a wolf on the fold"— nowadays high-school graduates don't recognize any of those lines, or the hundreds of others that used to paper the walls of the collective memory.

Only a few scraps remain. Students may know the first stanza of "The Highwayman," which comes in handy for teaching about metaphor. ("Is the poet saying that the moon was *really* a ghostly galleon?") They probably know Shelley's "Ozymandias," which makes for a good lesson about irony, not to mention the futility of big government. And they almost certainly know a bit of "Stopping by Woods on a Snowy Evening," which is pretty much the last poem left in the American literary canon—well, that, and "Casey at the Bat."

That obliteration was already well under way when I was in grade school, and I was spared some of its ravages only because I picked up the habit of memorizing poetry from my dad, who liked to recite to me when I was little—a mix of patriotic ballads like "Barbara Frietchie" and light verse by Don Marquis and the sadly forgotten Arthur Guiterman. I've tried to pass on some of these to my daughter, Sophie. She does an impressive job with the beginning of "The Cremation of Sam McGee," though she usually loses the track just after "mushing our way over the Dawson Trail."

But that's normal. Unless you're one of those freaks of nature who can soak this stuff up effortlessly, most of what you've got left of the poems you've learned is only snips and snatches—"My heart aches, and a something something pains my sense"; "I will arise and go now, and go to whatchamacallit"; "Ta tum ta tum, your mum and dad / They may not mean to but they do." Yet the odd thing is that once you've memorized a poem you still own it, even after you've forgotten most of the words and have to google it up the same way everyone else does.

That's reason enough for learning poems by heart, and there's no need to sully the case for memorization by claiming that it's good for mental discipline or cognitive development. Memorizing poetry does seem to make people a bit better at memorizing poetry, but there's no evidence that the skill carries over to other tasks.

For that matter, it's doubtful whether memorization makes you a better writer, either. Robert Pinsky once suggested that "anyone who has memorized a lot of poetry . . . [can't] fail to write coherent sentences and paragraphs." There's probably some truth to that nowadays, since the only people who know a lot of poetry by heart are the ones who were drawn to it out of a love of language. But the Victorian schoolchildren who learned reams of verse at the end of their teachers' canes grew up to write an awful lot of bad prose, most of it happily lost to literary memory.

It's misguided to wax nostalgic for a time when students were required to memorize sentimental ballads and patriotic rousers in the name of character building, and when kids who misbehaved were given twenty lines of poetry to learn as punishment. Memorization back then was a kind of conscription—the whole world learned to nod to a four-beat singsong: "The BOY stood ON the BURNing DECK / Whence ALL but HE had FLED."

The progressive educators of the twentieth century were right to want to sweep all that away. But they were wrong to dismiss memorization as mindless rote learning, as if the sounds alone communicated nothing by themselves. If you think you can understand poems without feeling them in your body, you're apt to treat them as no more than decorative op-ed pieces—you wind up teaching kids to value "The Road Not Taken" as merely a piece of sage advice about making difficult decisions.

I was about seven or eight years old when I learned Burns's "Scots wha' hae' wi' Wallace bled" from my dad. I had absolutely no idea what the poem was about or even what half the words meant—"Let him on wi' me"? But I learned something else—how verse can become a physical presence, in Robert Pinsky's words, which "operates at the borderland of body and mind."

That's an experience that you can only live fully when the poem comes from within rather than from the page in front of you. I like the way the Victorianist Catherine Robson put it: "When we don't learn by heart, the heart does not feel the rhythms of poetry as echoes of its own incessant beat."

REDSKIN BLUES

Fresh Air Commentary, June 14, 2005

=====

The Washington DC Court of Appeals will be ruling soon on a case involving a petition brought to cancel the trademark of the Washington Redskins on the grounds that the trademark law forbids the registration of marks that are disparaging. As it happens, I served pro bono as the linguistics expert for the seven Indians who brought the petition and wrote a report documenting the word's long history as an epithet, often a very nasty one.

One thing you won't find in that report, though, is a story that you often hear nowadays about where *redskin* comes from. As some people have been telling it, the word originally referred not to skin color, but to the bloody Indian scalps that whites paid bounties for. It's true that there's no way to tell for sure, since the origins of the word are lost in the late seventeenth century. But as best I can tell there's no historical record that connects *redskin* to the bounties for scalps, and in fact nobody seems to have mentioned the connection until about a dozen years ago. So it's almost certain that the word was originally a reference to skin color—after all, people refer to Indians as *the red man*, too, and that couldn't have anything to do with scalps. Not that Indians are really red, any more than people of other races are really white or black or yellow. But that Crayola theory of racial groupings runs very deep in our culture, and when kindergartners sit down at the play table, those are the crayons they reach for.

In a way, that story about *redskin* seems no different from the other tall tales that people pass around about word origins, what the linguist Larry Horn calls "etymythologies." There's the story that *posh* began as an acronym for "Port Out Starboard Home," the one about how *hooker* comes from the name of a Civil War general, or the one about how *son of a gun* originally referred to children born on the gun deck of a ship—all plausible-sounding, and all wrong.

You can find a whole collection of these tales in a very entertaining book by the etymologist Dave Wilton called *Word Myths*. Of course most of these stories aren't really myths in the narrow sense of the term—they're more on the order of little scraps of lexical romance that make a nice filler for the "Did You Know?" column of the Sunday newspaper. But the story about the origin of *redskin* is a myth in the deeper sense of the word. It's a story that's meant to illuminate a social truth, as if to say that the history of violence toward Indians is buried in the very words people use to talk about them.

You see a lot of stories like that one nowadays, attributing obscure and malignant origins to words relating to ethnic groups or sexual orientations. Look on the Web, and you'll find hundreds of pages relating how *faggot* is derived from the bundle of sticks that the medievals used when they burned homosexuals at the stake along with witches. But in fact *faggot* comes from an early-nineteenth-century word for a shrewish woman, which might derive from the image of something dry and brittle. And it wasn't until the beginning of the twentieth century that people started to use the word for male homosexuals.

Or take the story that *dyke* was derived from the name of the British queen Boudicca, who led a revolt against the Romans in the first century, and whose name became a synonym for a threatening woman. Actually the word only appeared in the 1930s and most likely comes from a version of *hermaphrodite*. And there's no truth either to the story that *handicap* refers to the idea that the disabled had to go begging, cap in hand. The word derives from a way of leveling the stakes for an uneven wager, where people put a certain amount of forfeit money in a hat. And it has been used of horse races since the mid-eighteenth century, whereas it's only in the past century or so that people have referred to disabled people as *the handicapped*.

For that matter, the phrase *rule of thumb* didn't originate with a law that said a man couldn't beat his wife with a stick that was any thicker than his thumb. And there's no more truth to the stories you hear that attribute racist origins to *picnic*, *crowbar*, and *the jig is up*.

I can understand why people find stories like these believable. Word histories can often be picaresque, and some words really did originate with ethnic or sexual slurs that are lost to memory now. *Gyp* comes from *Gypsy*, and *mollycoddle* comes from an old use of *molly* to mean a homosexual. Even the ordinary word *bad* probably originated with an Anglo-Saxon disparagement for an effeminate man.

But it doesn't really matter where any of these words came from. Since Plato's time, people have thought of words as carrying around their origins like original sin, as if some long-forgotten sense could still have the power to infect their meanings. But if *redskin* and the rest are ugly words today, it's not because they bear some hidden historical taint—it's because they conjure up ugly ideas that are still with us.

WORD OF THE YEAR

Fresh Air Commentary, December 13, 2006

The business of naming a "word of the year" began as a half-whimsical exercise in 1990, when the members of the American Dialect Society decided at their annual meeting to pick the word that best encapsulated some feature of the prevailing Zeitgeist. Within a few years, the press was picking up on the vote as a cute end-of-the-year feature, and dictionary publishers and others began to get into the act, with an eye to getting some free publicity.

This year's winners are already trickling in. The Oxford American Dictionary chose the expression *carbon neutral*, and the linguist Dennis Baron picked *roadside bomb* at his Web of Language Web site. But while both those terms have been in the headlines, they aren't particularly interesting as words in themselves, no more than *bird flu* or *polonium*. Webster's *New World Dictionary* named *crackberry*, which actually peaked in 2000, when Karl Rove was using his Blackberry to dispatch messages to the Republican troops with both thumbs—the word seems a little arrière-garde six years later, when Research in Motion is fighting to hold on to its market share.

A better choice might be *truthiness*, which Merriam-Webster named as 2006 word of the year on the basis of an online survey. The only problem is that it's the same word the American Dialect Society picked for 2005, and not even Stephen Colbert should get to win two years running for the same performance.

Anyway, those are merely the Golden Globes and People's Choice awards of lexicography. Serious wordinistas will be waiting for the linguistic Oscars, when the American Dialect Society makes its selection in January.

It's a strong field this year, what with contenders like *Islamo-fascism*, *netroots*, *dwarf planet*, *buzzkill*, and *the decider*. Or if you were looking simply for the most bounce to the ounce, you might decide to go with *macaca*, an item whose first and only appearance in American public discourse could be credited with tipping the Senate to the Democrats. Given the razor-thin margin in the Virginia Senate race, it's a fair bet that George Allen would have kept his seat if not for the flap when he used the word to refer to an Indian American at a campaign rally and then tried to explain it away as a term he'd made up on the spot without knowing what it meant. If that was so, it was certainly a bit of freakish bad luck that led him to tumble on a word that happens to be a racial slur in the North African French spoken by his mother.

But in that case, maybe the nod should go to another career-derailing racial slur that found its way via YouTube into the national spotlight. True, the career in question wasn't nearly as high-flying as Allen's. Before his meltdown at LA's Laugh Factory, people rarely referred to Michael Richards without adding, "you know, the guy who played Kramer on Seinfeld." But that's just what made the uproar so notable from a purely linguistic point of view. Here's a B-list celebrity who lurches into an incoherent racist diatribe in the middle of a nightclub standup routine. And the next thing you know he's all over the media and making the customary circuit of public contrition with Letterman and Jesse Jackson, delivering himself of the turgid self-analysis that betrays a life spent in acting classes: "I was in a place of humiliation. . . . I need to get into the depths of my being." It was as if Richards was the only person who didn't understand that nobody remotely cared what kind of place he was in when he went into his rampage. The whole business was simply a pretext for giving audiences another chance to watch the mesmerizing spectacle of someone giving in to the rage that's implicit in that word. "Oh my God," you could hear a woman say as Richards launched into his tirade, and that pretty much summed up most people's reaction. Of course everybody knows the word, but nowadays most middle-class whites have suppressed it as a redneck vulgarity. So it was a shock to hear it yelled as a venomous insult, particularly by the endearingly rambunctious character who used to come crashing through Jerry's open door every week.

No, we can't ban the word, but we can't easily pretend we've gotten past it, either. "I'm not a racist," Richards said, with apparently genuine puzzlement. But that's the thing about that word—whatever you think your intentions are, it trails its own history of hate and violence into the room. That's why Richards's outburst led some black comics like Paul Mooney to announce that they'd be dropping the word from their own material from now on.

Of course this particular epithet has been in the running for word of the year before. It could have been selected in 1998, when black leaders threatened to boycott Merriam-Webster for not beginning its dictionary definition of the word by labeling it as offensive. Or in 1995, when a tape of Detective Mark Fuhrman using the word was played at the O.J. trial, reinforcing the jury's suspicion that the LA police might have planted evidence.

Or if the linguists had been voting back then, the word could have been chosen in 1988, when the group NWA or Niggaz With Attitude brought gangsta rap into the musical mainstream with their album *Straight Outta Compton* and set off an ongoing controversy over the use of the word by black entertainers. Or in 1966, when Lady Bird Johnson asked the US Board on Geographic Names to change the name of Nigger Head Mountain near Burnet, Texas.

Or before that, in 1948, when Strom Thurmond ran for president as a Dixiecrat and told his audiences that not all the troops in the army could "force the southern people to break down segregation and admit the nigger race into our theatres into our swimming pools into our homes and into our churches." Or in 1928, when Paul Robeson was criticized for singing the word in the lyrics to "Old Man River" in a production of the Kern-Hammerstein musical *Show Boat*.*

---

*The original version of the lyrics began: "Niggers all work on de Mississippi / Niggers all work while de white folks play. . . . " When Robeson sang the words in the 1928 London production of the play, Harlem's *Amsterdam News* said, "If anyone were to call him a 'nigger' he'd be the first to get offended, and there he is singing 'nigger, nigger' before all those white people." The word was omitted from later versions of the musical, which tended to soft-pedal its racial themes and to play it as a colorful costume drama about the old South. For the 1936 film version, "niggers" was changed to "darkies," and then to "colored folks" in the 1946 Broadway revival. That in turn became "Here we all work on the Mississippi" when Frank Sinatra sang the song in white tails in *Till the Clouds Roll By*, Arthur Freed's 1946 film biography of Jerome Kern. And by the time Freed made his 1951 film version of *Show Boat*, the chorus was cut entirely.

Actually, that's precisely why it's unlikely that anybody will choose the epithet as the word of the year for 2006. The Richards episode may have been shocking, but it didn't really tell us anything we didn't know already. And if history is any guide, you can be sure the word will be back in contention for the honor in years to come.

SIZE DOESN'T MATTER

Fresh Air Commentary, April 18, 2006

═══════

At any one moment there are thousands of bogus statistics floating around in the media, and fully 37 percent of them have to do with language. There are 40 million Americans who speak no English. Communication is 90 percent nonverbal. Eskimo has 87 different words for snow. If you believe any of that, I've got an Inuit thesaurus I'd like to sell you.

But the media have an endless and uncritical appetite for these nuggets, particularly when they seem to confirm some cherished linguistic lore. And there's no shortage of hucksters ready to satisfy that need. Take one Paul J. J. Payack, a California marketing executive who has a gift for concocting appealing factoids about language trends. Back in February, for example, Payack announced that, using a secret algorithm, he had determined that the English language contained exactly 986,120 words, and that it would pass the million mark this fall.

The item got wide coverage—it was picked up by sources from the *New York Times* to Reuters to NPR. And it does have a certain Googlish plausibility to it. With all this stuff out there on the Web, you might conclude that you can count pretty much anything. But Payack is simply blowing smoke. For one thing, no third party can determine how many distinct word-forms a search engine like Google or Yahoo! has indexed in its database. And even if you knew that, there would be no easy way to tell how many different words you're dealing with. Is *play* the same word when it refers to a theater play, a baseball play, fair play, and a stock-market play? Is it the same word in playing the violin, playing third base, and playing someone for a sucker? Is *player* different words when it refers to Barry Bonds and Puffy Combs?

Then too, not even the Web allows you to eavesdrop on every conversation in every nook and cranny of the English-speaking world. When it comes to the crunch, trying to count the words of the language is as futile an exercise as trying to determine exactly how many socks Americans lost in 2005. But Payack's claim bestows a satisfying statistical patina on a familiar story about the glorious amplitude of English. People never tire of boasting that English has more words than any other language. And they invariably go on to praise the openness and flexibility of the language and the marvelous expressiveness and richness of vocabulary that have made it the envy of lesser tongues.

Granted, our dictionaries can lick their dictionaries. Merriam-Webster's *Third International* clocks in at around half a million words, against a mere 150,000 for the biggest dictionaries the French or Russians can come up with. But that doesn't mean we have more words for the things that matter. Once you get past 50,000 words or so, you're strictly in crossword puzzle territory—and I mean the hard ones that the *New York Times* runs toward the end of the week. The page of Webster's *Third International* that contains the word *okay* lists about 120 entries in all. But only half a dozen or so are words that you might actually hear in conversation, like *ointment, old,* and *oink.* The rest are items like *oinochoe, oka,* and *oke,* which if you'll cast your mind back are respectively the words for an ancient Greek wine pitcher, a cheese made by Canadian Trappist monks, and a unit of weight used in Turkey and Egypt.

And that's not to mention all those fish names: *oilfish; o'io,* the Hawaiian bonefish; *olisthops,* an Australian herring; and *oldwife,* which, depending on where you're sitting down to dinner, can be a kind of bream, triggerfish, perch, shad, or pompano. Over the centuries, English speakers have planted their flags beside a lot of different waters, and they've always found a use for the poles afterwards. But it's unlikely that the vision of a language with 5,000 fish names probably would have ignited envy in the heart of García Lorca or Kafka (it might have moved Flaubert).

There's an anachronistic vanity in the satisfaction we take in our swollen wordbooks, as if English speakers in Des Moines are enriched every time someone in Dublin or Delhi coins a new slang word for a ne'er-do-well. It's the last residue of the imperial pride that used to swell in British bosoms at the contemplation of all the bits of the map that were colored pink.

Of course nowadays it's only the English language that the sun never sets on, and we're more likely to take that as a tribute to our charm than to our global power. That explains the appeal of another of Mr. Payack's factoids: according to his algorithms, he says, the most frequently spoken word on the planet is *okay.* More humbug. It isn't easy to say what the most frequently spoken word on the planet is—most likely it's a toss-up between English *the* and the Chinese particle *de*. But it's unlikely that *okay* would even make the top thousand. In fact *okay* is far from being the most widely diffused English word—that honor would probably go to either *Coca-Cola* or *CIA*.

But there's something comforting in the idea that *okay* is America's most successful linguistic export—it lets us believe that the triumph of English reflects the allure of our popular culture rather than our economic or political clout. This is a story about Tom Hanks, not Halliburton. Whatever the world may think about our policies, they like us—they really, really like us.

THE STYLE IS THE MAG

Fresh Air Commentary, March 22, 2007

In its eighty-fourth year, *Time* magazine has just given itself a face-lift, with a new look and revamped content. Along the way, the editors announced that they'll be getting rid of the last vestiges of the involuted syntax that used to be a stylistic signature of the mag: "Died. Charles ('Pretty Boy') Floyd, desperado, of gunshot wounds, near East Liverpool, Ohio."

Actually, it has been a long time since inverted sentences like that were prominent in *Time* outside of its "Milestones" section. If people remember that particular tic today, it's mostly via a famous line from a parody of *Time* that Wolcott Gibbs wrote in the *New Yorker* in 1936: "Backwards ran sentences until reeled the mind." But there was a lot more to *Time*-style than that, back when the magazine was transforming journalism with a new and compelling tone of voice.

The style was originally the creation of Briton Hadden, who cofounded *Time* with Henry Luce in 1923. The two were right out of Yale, and the magazine's language was laced with the airs and affectations of a bright undergraduate. The vocabulary was a showy mix of the exotic, the folksy, and the contrived—anything that might suggest an arch detachment from the subject. *Time* popularized esoteric foreign words like the Hindi *pundit* and turned the Japanese-derived *tycoon* into a familiar word for a magnate. It adapted the Greek word *kudos* as a synonym for *praise* (originally the word meant simply "glory"). It revived archaic and dialect words like *hustings*, *hornswoggle*, *passel*, and *scrivener*. And it contributed a long list of breezy coinings to the language, from early items like *pinko*, *newshawk*, *socialite*, *pollster*, and *racketeer* to later terms like *Disneyfication*, *eco-freak*, and *televangelist*.

In *Time*-style, people never walked—they sauntered, strode, shambled, ambled, or slouched. And they made their entries preceded by a retinue of Homeric epithets, sometimes lined up two or three deep—"gaunt, scraggle-haired President Eamon de Valera," "burly but suave Benito Mussolini," "sloe-eyed, soft-spoken Generalissimo Francisco Franco." Tall, lanky men were invariably *Lincolnesque*—at one time or another the adjective was applied to Henry Wallace, Raymond Massey, Henry Fonda, Omar Bradley, Arthur Miller, Gregory Peck, and Anthony Perkins. And the writers ransacked the thesaurus for descriptions of Hermann Göring's girth—over the course of the 1930s his name was prefixed by *bull-necked*, *beefy*, *big-boned*, *obese*, *stanch-bellied*, and *porcine*.

That language was aimed at turning the people *Time* wrote about into the stock characters of miniature B-movie melodramas, each with its setup, angle, twist, and final kicker. The template rarely varied. People often repeat the Count de Buffon's remark that "the style is the man," but at *Time*, the style was the mag. It could boast a brilliant stable of writers—its early alumni included Stephen Vincent Benét, James Agee, John O'Hara, and Archibald MacLeish. But they had to submit to an editorial process that extirpated any trace of individuality. To *Time*'s critics, that process stood in for the magazine's pernicious influence on journalism in general. In 1957, Garry Wills wrote that *Time*'s mass-produced style was creating a kind of Newspeak, by collectivizing language and thought. And Marshall McLuhan described *Time*'s style as a language in which nobody could tell the truth.

Those concerns seem remote now. For one thing, *Time*'s journalism is much better now, and its politics have softened since the days when liberal Democrats wouldn't let the magazine cross their doorstep. In any case, *Time* doesn't have the political or cultural importance it did in its early decades—now it's just another publication fighting for its life as its paper shrivels up from under it. And the magazine has long since abandoned the flash and brummagem of its early style, along with its impersonality. *Time* has been giving its writers credit for forty years now, and the first-person pronoun is no longer a stranger to its pages. When we run across a bit of clever wordplay now, we know whom to thank for it. In a recent review, Richard Corliss described the display of buff male bodies in *300* as "Homer eroticism." It's a bit that would have done credit to *Time* in its heyday, but it reads better with a byline under it than it would have as the product of an anonymous style-machine.

But much of *Time*-style hasn't so much disappeared as it has been absorbed into the zero-degree communal language of modern journalism. There are the background descriptions that set the scene: "As a thin rain fell on Washington last week. . . . " There are the punning headers: a 1934 story about the frantic efforts to finish the Moscow subway on schedule for the Soviet five-year plan was called "Planic Rush," and one about a low turnout in a vote among farmers on corn-hog subsidies was called "Half Hog"—the sorts of headers that are routine these days in publications from *Barron's* to the *New Republic.* More important, *Time* shaped the pervasive tone of modern journalism—knowing, distanced, superior, and a little cynical.

In the old days, critics sometimes professed to see an inconsistency between the cockiness and irreverence of *Time's* style and its editorial deference to success and power—one writer described the style as embodying an ethical schizophrenia. But that got it dead wrong. As *Time* used them, archness and irony were devices for accommodating and diminishing the more unpleasant realities of the world. Edmund Wilson once said that *Time's* style reduced human beings to manikins—it gave the impression that "the pursuits, past and present, of the human race are rather an absurd little scandal about which you might find out some even nastier details if you met the editors of *Time* over cocktails." Wilson wouldn't have been that hard on *Time* itself today. But I wonder what he would have had to say about cable news.

INDECENT EXPOSURE

Fresh Air Commentary, June 13, 2007

═══

Whichever side of the issue you were on, you might have been disconcerted by the language of the statement that the Federal Communications Commission chair Kevin Martin posted on the agency's Web site after the New York Court of Appeals threw out the FCC's indecency rulings against the Fox network for broadcasting what the court called "fleeting expletives."

Martin's statement began, "I find it hard to believe that the New York court would tell American families that 'shit' and 'fuck' are fine to say on broadcast television." He went on to warn that the decision would give Hollywood free rein to say anything they want to whenever they like, managing to repeat *shit* and *fuck* half a dozen times in the course of five short paragraphs.

It's hard to imagine an FCC chairman from some earlier era using those words with such gusto. Traditionalist or no, Martin is clearly not a man who has much use for old-fashioned demurrals like "decency forbids me" or "I blush to repeat." It puts you in mind of those cable news shows where the host and guests fulminate over the coarsening of American culture against a backdrop of strategically blurred *Girls Gone Wild* videos.

On the surface, Martin's indignation seemed disproportionate to the rather technical legal point at issue. The court held that when you use a word like *fucking* as a mere intensifier, the way people had on the Fox programs, it doesn't have any sexual meaning, so can't be indecent in the legal sense of the term. Nonsense, said Martin and the FCC. The f-word has a sexual connotation whenever it's used.

The agency's critics had a lot of fun with that position. The political blogger Daniel Drezner asked, "Am I obviously encouraging rape and bestiality when I say 'F#$% Kevin Martin and the horse he rode in on'?"

Still, Martin does have a point. Even when the words aren't literally indecent, they have lubricious overtones that can make them offensive. After all, it isn't simply a phonetic accident that that the words we use as insults and intensifiers sound just like the ones we use to talk about sex and elimination. This isn't like being put out simply because you hear somebody on the radio describing Glenn Gould as a pianist.

None of that should blur the legal distinction. Overtones or no, there's still a difference between indecency and cussing, between the obscene and the merely vulgar. But as Martin understands very well, this has a lot more to do with symbolic politics than with legalities or practical consequences. It's not as if anybody really believes that the youth of America are going to be corrupted by hearing an occasional f- or s-word on a broadcast. In fact the members of my own generation mastered the fine subtleties of linguistic depravity with no help from the media at all.

But Americans are widely troubled by what they correctly perceive as an increase in public swearing and profanity, whether it's indecent or merely vulgar. In a 2002 Public Agenda survey of attitudes about civility sponsored by the Pew Foundation, 84 percent of respondents said that it bothered them when people use bad or rude language out in public, and three-quarters wanted parents to teach their kids that "cursing is always wrong."

There's no shortage of theories about who deserves the blame. As Martin and other culture warriors tell it, foul language is just a stand-in for all the depredations that Hollywood, the media, and the cultural elites have been visiting on American families since the sexualization of America got under way in the 1960s. From that point of view, this is just the latest episode in what the historian Rochelle Gurstein calls the "repeal of reticence," as people progressively abandoned the old inhibitions about the public discussion of sexuality, the body, and the intimate details of personal life. Trace those expletives back to their source, the story goes, and they'll take you to *Oh! Calcutta!* and *Fear of Flying*, Jerry Rubin and Lenny Bruce, and further still to *Lady Chatterley's Lover*, *Ulysses*, and all the avant-garde assaults on traditional standards of propriety and decency.

But forty years after the sexual revolution began in earnest, you still don't hear these words used much in the media in their literal sexual meanings, or at least outside of a Chris Rock routine or an episode of *Deadwood* on pay cable. What you hear instead is the parallel vocabulary of vulgarisms that emerged over the last century, as people transformed all the venerable English obscenities into terms of abuse. The a-word became a name for an arrogant jerk, the s-word for a nasty creep, the bs-word for meretricious humbug. And the infinitely versatile f-word was deployed not just as an all-purpose intensifier, but as the basis for new verbs meaning "cheat," "meddle," "tease," "betray," and "bungle," among other things.

But the spread of that vocabulary owes nothing to the media or the cultural elites. It was invented early in the century by working-class men, and it took root in American speech when millions of middle-class inductees brought it home after World War II. And though it too entered the linguistic mainstream in the '60s, it ultimately had no more political significance than long hair or rock music did. Whoever uses it, it's simply a way of signaling attitude or street—"a demonstration of earthy authenticity," as Charles Krauthammer approvingly described Dick Cheney's anatomically challenging imperative to Pat Leahy on the Senate floor a few years ago.

This language really belongs to all of us, as Kevin Martin more or less acknowledged when he laced his statement with it. But unlike the explicitly sexual vocabulary that it followed into the open, it doesn't really threaten old-fashioned sexual values. On the contrary, the words can only work in their figurative meanings if they remain dirty in their literal meanings. If there's still an aggressive intensity to calling somebody a fucking asshole, it's because we haven't abandoned our conviction that sex and the body are something to be ashamed of. You'd hope the champions of decency would take some comfort in that.

THE REGRESSIVE URGE

Fresh Air Commentary, August 16, 2007

Not long ago, *Newsweek* ran a guest column by an Alabama college professor who was complaining about his students' sloppy writing—one of those familiar language diatribes that seem to come with the system disk. Whenever a student hands in a paper with the words "It goes without saying," he says, he scribbles in the margin, "Then why say it?"

Nobody gets through life without having an English teacher like that, though if you're lucky you'll get yours out of the way well before you reach college. Mine was Mrs. Bosch in the eighth grade. Let someone hand in a paper with the sentence, "Having been thrown in the air, the dog caught the stick," and Mrs. Bosch would dispatch the writer before the entire class with pointed sarcasm: "Why, the poor animal!" And we would crack up, partly out of sadistic pleasure at the humiliation visited on our hapless classmate and partly because it pleased us to be let in on the joke.

Mrs. Bosch's sarcasm was a crucial part of our education as writers, such as it was—her sharp voice was an inward presence as we scanned our words, trying to make sure their meanings at least vaguely coincided with what we were trying to say.

And of course she had our eighth-grade number. That's the age when kids are all going a little crazy with the discovery of sarcasm, as they realize the power of echoing someone else's words or thoughts in a way that makes them sound deluded or foolish. In the school yard sarcasm replaces brute insult, as kids move from "you butthead retard" to "smooth move, guy." And it's their first line of defense against parental authority, as they learn to voice their grudging compliance in a tone that makes their disaffection clear: "Yeah, *right*, Dad."

Adolescent sarcasm can be irritating—that's what it's supposed to be—but we can look on it a little indulgently; after all, what else have thirteen-year-olds got going for them? But when grown people engage in it, it can come off as disconcertingly juvenile.

Yet when the subject of language comes up, a lot of people revert to a tone of sarcastic mockery that hasn't deepened a whit since they were in middle school. Take the piece that Dick Cavett wrote about the decline of English for the Web-based *New York Times* Select in August 2007. Cavett began by warning that we're losing our grip on our glorious English language and proceeded to roll off a series of familiar japes about mispronunciations of *heinous* and *nuclear*, not to mention that chestnut about *literally* that my Mrs. Bosch performed for three generations of middle-schoolers: "'The senator literally exploded with laughter.' And *who* cleaned up the mess?"

When a flight attendant announces, "We will be landing in Chicago momentarily," Cavett says, he enjoys replying, "Will there be time to get off?" Actually, I have trouble imagining that that exchange ever took place. I mean, Cavett makes his little witticism, and the flight attendant gives him this look that says, "Excuse me?" and then he has to explain, "Oh, I was merely venturing a jocular reference to the prescriptive grammarians' insistence that the adverb *momentarily* should be used only to signify 'for a moment' rather than 'in a moment.'" I can't see it—my guess is that if Cavett actually replied to that announcement, it was sotto voce to an imaginary companion. But the gag tells better this way. As Mrs. Bosch understood full well, the point of sarcasm isn't just to humiliate the clueless—it's also for the benefit of an audience who are in on the joke. That's who teenagers are appealing to with their eye-rolls, as if they were glancing over to an invisible homey in the other corner of the room.

You could sense the same yearning for solidarity among the eight hundred or so readers who posted online comments to Cavett's piece, the majority of them with a sarcastic take on some usage that sears their ears or has them screaming at their TV set: "What do you mean 'broad daylight'? Could it happen in 'narrow daylight'?" "As for those who 'feel badly,' I believe they refer to an impaired tactile sense."

It's easy to dismiss this humor as sophomoric—and even that might involve skipping a grade or two. But it answers to a simple desire for communion with others who know better. And in its own way it leaves you with a reassuring sense of complacency about the state of English. These complaints may always be bracketed by apocalyptic warnings about the imminent collapse of the language, but if the greatest linguistic threats we're facing are things like the confusion of *prone* and *supine* and a shaky grasp on the *lie/lay* distinction, then we'll probably muddle through. It's like hearing someone warn of grave domestic security threats and then learning that he's chiefly concerned about Canadian sturgeon-poaching on the US side of Lake Huron.

In fact the inconsequentiality of those issues belies the charges of elitism that critics are always leveling at the wordinistas. Think of the way Lynne Truss has ridden this shtick to the top of the best-seller lists: with operatic indignation, she draws millions of readers into a sense of confraternity with everybody else who got the possessive rule down cold in middle school. What could be more democratic than that? Language may be infinitely deep and mysterious, but when it comes to mastery of the apostrophe, you and I can walk hand in hand with Henry James.

PUTTIN' ON THE STYLE

Fresh Air Commentary, March 17, 2008

The death of William F. Buckley last month sent the writers of obituaries and appreciations to their dictionaries in search of Buckleyisms they could drop in by way of homage. The *New York Times* headed its page-one obituary "William F. Buckley Jr., 82, Dies: Sesquipedalian Spark of Right." Not surprisingly, that mystified quite a few readers, particularly since the article underneath it didn't give the game away until paragraph 24, where it finally let on that *sesquipedalian* means "characterized by the use of long words." Still, if you're going to have people scratching their heads over a word in somebody's obituary, whose better than Buckley's?

I counted more than a dozen of these stories that used the word *sesquipedalian*, though most weren't as coy as the *Times* about explaining the word. In *Newsweek*, Evan Thomas described Buckley as "a lover of big words (a sesquipedalian, as he might say)." And indeed Buckley did call himself that on occasion (though unlike Thomas, he knew that *sesquipedalian* can only be an adjective—it's not a noun like *Episcopalian*). The word is particularly apt for him, and not just because of his fondness for polysyllables. It was coined by the Roman poet Horace, who referred slightingly to poets who use *sesquipedalia verba*, which literally means words a foot and a half long. The word was Horace's little joke, an example of the very thing it was ridiculing, and it has been tinged with mockery ever since. So it accords nicely with the slightly self-mocking persona that Buckley fashioned for himself. The slouch, the drawling patrician voice, the arching eyebrows, and the darting lizard tongue—it all served to avert the irritation that a highfalutin vocabulary might otherwise have engendered. We Americans tend to be tough on erudition that's untempered by humor, at least when it comes from one of our own. Unfairly or not, we'll tax George Will with pedantry for using a word that we'll receive with an indulgent smile when it comes from Christopher Hitchens. Use a fancy word in public, and you risk being accused of affectation, elitism, or simply what people used to call "puttin' on the style."

With the exception of Senator Pat Moynihan, I can't think of any modern public figure but Buckley who managed to allay those impressions while still getting people to take him and his language seriously. David Frye and Robin Williams could get his voice dead-on, but his verbal style is surprisingly hard to capture, even for those who were close to him. In his appreciation of Buckley, *National Review*'s Jonah Goldberg described him affectionately as "the peripatetic proselytizer of polysyllabism." But that doesn't sound like Buckley—it's more reminiscent of Spiro Agnew disgorging one of those prefabricated chunks like "nattering nabobs of negativism" that his speechwriter William Safire used to cook up for him. It's the same sort of thing that Bill O'Reilly does when he overenunciates words like *bloviate* and *opine*—a big-word buffoonery that actually implies a disdain for language. These are people who choose their words as if they were shopping for lawn ornaments.

There are people do this polysyllabic wordplay engagingly— Safire, for example, ever since he's been filing under his own byline. But this is just a weekend diversion for Safire; he doesn't talk that way on *Meet the Press*. Whereas Buckley's devotion to recondite words was profound and passionate—and sometimes immoderate. Word collectors always have to tread a fine line between flattering their readers' erudition and basking in their own, and Buckley couldn't always keep his balance. He had a weakness for what the critic H. W. Fowler described as "Wardour Street words," after the street in Soho where Londoners used to shop for decorative bric-a-brac. He couldn't resist using *catechize* in place of *question* or *grill*, *vaticination* for *forecast*, *estop* for *stop*, and *eo ipso* for *in and of itself.*

Of course he would have said that those words had nuances that were absent in their everyday synonyms, and that using them encouraged people to stretch their vocabularies. He wrote once that asking someone to avoid uncommon words is like "advising a composer that he may not use diminished chords in his next symphony." That's fair enough. But reading Buckley, you sometimes wished that he had confined his composing to the white keys. "A flotilla of missiles could be estopped in mid-air"—did *estopped* really do something there that *stopped* wouldn't have?

Or take the time he worked *albescent* into a description of the sea in an account he wrote for *People* in 1980 about crossing the Atlantic in a sailboat. It was an elegant touch, particularly for readers of the magazine whose Latin was up to recognizing that the word meant "whitish." But even for them, *albescent* doesn't conjure up a specific shade of white the way a concrete word like *chalk* or *frost* or *ivory* does. That's the price you pay for using sesquipedalian words—the higher they soar, the more remote they are from the world of concrete feeling and sensation on the ground below. And as Horace said, you have to set them aside if you want to touch the heart.

Buckley had trouble renouncing that language, and the failure came at a cost. His penchant for lexical bling-bling helped make him a cultural personage, but it also left him a lesser writer than his gifts might have enabled him to become. Still, the woods are full of gifted writers, and there was only one of him.

PAUSE FOR THOUGHT

Fresh Air Commentary, April 14, 2008

━━━━━━━━

I always find it disconcerting to hear a tape of myself having a conversation or giving a talk—do I really say *um* that much? Of course we tune out all our own tics and twitches when we're speaking, but nothing makes you seem quite as scattered as those *ums* do. Pause silently in mid-utterance, and you sound deliberate and thoughtful. Drop an *um* into the pause, and you sound hesitant, indecisive, or simply dim. As the author of an early twentieth-century book on public speaking expressed his condemnation of the word: "Grunting is no part of thinking."

Letter for letter, *um* probably comes in for more disdain than any other item in the English vocabulary. I say "item" because most people won't even do *um* the dignity of calling it a word—some actually get offended when they find out it's listed in the dictionary. It seems more like a meaningless noise we use to fill out our hesitations, like the hum your hard drive makes while it's trying to retrieve a big file.

But like it or not, *um* is clearly a word of English. Speakers of other languages signal their hesitation very differently. In

Mandarin you say *neige*, in Japanese you say *eeto* or *ano*, and in American Sign Language you circle your forearm with your palm up and your fingers spread. In fact English-speaking children have to learn to use *um* and *uh*, just as they have to learn *ball* or *drink* or *please*. The only difference is that when you say *um* and *uh*, you're not referring to anything in the world but commenting on your own utterance. That's what makes the words fascinating to psychologists and linguists who are trying to figure out how we turn our thoughts into language.

For a very readable account of all this research you can turn to a recent book by the science writer Michael Erard with the easy-to-remember title *Um*. The book actually covers a range of speech slips and blunders from spoonerisms to Bushisms, but it's particularly interesting on what you could think of as the umological paradox. On the one hand, *um* and *uh* seem to play a useful communicative role. According to the psychologists Herb Clark and Jean Fox Tree, speakers use the words to signal upcoming delays in speech—*uh* for a minor delay and *um* for a major one. Depending on the context, those signals might mean that the speaker wants to hold the floor, needs time to search for a word, or has to stop and go back to repair a mispronunciation or mistake.

But as useful as it may be, people have been putting the knock on *um* for centuries. It was the sixteenth-century versions of *um* and *uh* that gave rise to the expression "hem and haw" for dithering. And the criticism of *um* has become more insistent over the modern period, as we've turned the word into what Erard calls the emblem of a disorganized mind.

Maybe the problem with *um* is that it draws attention to our disfluencies and hesitations. That's especially noticeable when it's used in a context that ordinarily calls for a certain amount of deliberation. Fillers and false starts tend to pass right by us in casual conversation, but they can become maddeningly distracting when we hear somebody using them in a radio interview or political debate. And you could argue that modern broadcast media have made us more alert to the overuse of *um* than ever before.

But even as we condemn *um* as an unconscious mark of hesitation, we find it useful to have around when we want to consciously fake that effect. People have always used *um* to introduce a euphemism or circumlocution, as if they were halted by a sudden twinge of delicacy—"I'll spare you a recap of last night's, um, unpleasantness." And over the past few years we've started to see a new use of the word, as a mock apology before you correct somebody who says something particularly stupid or does something inappropriate. As in "Um, actually, Ringo was the band's drummer." Or "Um, we don't use that word around here."

You run into that pseudo-deferential *um* all over the place these days, not just in speech but in email, blogs, and news features. It has become a hallmark of a hip style of writing that affects the spontaneity of real-time communication, hesitations and all. And the new *um* suggests a certain shift in attitude, too. You could think of it as a replacement for the snippy *hello* that first caught on in the 1980s. That too was used to emphasize someone's utter cluelessness: "HelLO? Ringo was the band's *drummer!*" But the tone is completely different. *HelLO* oozes condescending ridicule—"Is anybody home?"—whereas *um* involves a more subtle maneuver. You profess a polite hesitation to embarrass or confront the person you're correcting, but that makes it pointedly clear that the person has good reason to be chagrined.

I don't imagine that a lot of people will miss that sarcastic *hello* when it's finally put out to pasture. And I suppose you could see the apologetic *um* as the harbinger of a new age of ostensible civility. But that isn't exactly the sign of a kindlier, gentler English language. All that the new *um* really shows is just how snarky civility can be.

UNDER THE BUS

Fresh Air Commentary, April 22, 2008

═══════════

To judge from the media, the presidential candidates have been spending half their time extenuating their own mistakes and the other half repudiating the things said and done by their supporters and friends. So it's not surprising the phrase *under the bus* has appeared in more than four hundred press stories on the campaign over the last six months. Under the bus is where Hillary was described as throwing her chief strategist, Mark Penn, and where the radio talk show host Bill Cunningham said John McCain had thrown him after McCain disavowed Cunningham's reference to "Barack Hussein Obama" at a McCain rally. And after Barack Obama's speech on race, under the bus is where he was accused of throwing his grandmother by Ann Coulter, Fred Barnes, Rich Lowry, and Karl Rove, not to mention well over a hundred other conservative columnists and bloggers. That piling on might suggest a certain lack of originality. But not many people could pass up an opportunity to charge a politician they don't like with throwing his grandmother under a bus, even if it's only in a manner of speaking.

That helps to explain why *throw someone under the bus* has shot so quickly from new kid on the block to the idiom A-list. The word sleuth Grant Barrett has traced it back as early as 1991, but its origins are lost in the mists of the 1980s.

Some people suggest it's derived from a phrase for a washed-up rock star on tour, and others connect it to the announcement made by a minor-league baseball manager: "Bus leaving. Be on it or under it." There's no evidence for either origin. But we always assume that there has to be some real-life scenario behind each of these metaphors, however far-fetched it is, and the internet and bookstore shelves are teeming with treasure troves of word lore eager to oblige us with ingenious speculations. As in: "See, back in Elizabethan times the household pets used to curl up in the thatched roofs to keep warm until they were washed out by a downpour, and ever since then. . . . "

You hear a lot of talk these days about the wisdom of crowds, but when it comes to the crunch, we're reluctant to credit the collective mind with the same creative imagination that we accord to an individual artist. It's as if we expected Bob Dylan to be able to point to the event that inspired every line in his songs: "Well, we were on this camping trip and trying to figure out which way to pitch our tents to keep the wind out. So I wet my finger and stuck it in the air, and I said. . . ."

Actually, it's my guess that somebody just pulled *throw under the bus* out of the ether one day, and other people picked it up and passed it along. It's what marketers like to describe as a viral process, except that these aren't exactly like the mysterious fads that can instantaneously populate every kindergarten class with Ethans and Emmas. The geography of betrayal is already mapped out pretty thoroughly in English: you can hang someone out to dry, throw him to the wolves, let him twist in the wind, sell him down the river, offer him up as a scapegoat, or make him a fall guy, a patsy, or a sacrificial lamb. So *throw under the bus* couldn't have caught on unless it suggested a compelling new take on familiar perfidies.

Or probably I should say new takes, since the expression seems to conjure up different things for different people. Some think of the thrower and throwee as fellow passengers on a team bus or tour bus. That would explain why we talk about *the* bus rather than *a* bus, and it foregrounds the idea of a betrayal. But it makes the action a little hard to picture, since you have to imagine one rider on a moving bus managing to throw another rider under its wheels, which seems like a stunt from a Steven Seagal movie. So evidently a lot of people just picture the victim being pushed off a curb in front of an oncoming Greyhound. But one way or the other, the expression conveys a singularly modern image of stop-at-nothing ruthlessness.

These things work like little film clips. You hear, "He made her take the fall," and you flash on *The Maltese Falcon*; you hear, "He threw her under the bus," and you envision some more recent movie—I don't know exactly how the plot goes, but you can be sure the camera won't cut away at the moment of impact.

We have more exacting standards in mayhem these days, whether in our movies or our metaphors. There was a time when the emblematic moment of movie sadism was Jimmy Cagney shoving a half-grapefruit into Mae Clarke's face in *The Public Enemy*, and when people could still get a vicarious tingle out of saying that so-and-so got worked over or got the living daylights beat out of him.

But those expressions seem pretty demure for the age of Hannibal Lecter and the pneumatic cattle gun that Javier Bardem wields in *No Country for Old Men*. The verbal violence that we get off on is a lot more graphic, which is why Google reports nearly a quarter of a million hits for *ripping somebody a new one*.

I have some trouble imagining Cagney using that phrase, probably for the same reason it's hard to picture Sam Spade telling Bridget O'Shaughnessy, "Angel, I'm throwing you under the bus." Every age seems to get the idioms it deserves.

PLAYING POLITICS

THE LANGUAGE OF ABUSE

Fresh Air Commentary, May 13, 2004

═══════

"Torture is torture is torture," Secretary of State Colin Powell pronounced in an interview on *Fox News Sunday* with Chris Wallace, in a nice demonstration of how tautologies can counter moral relativism. But that depends on what paper you read. The press in France, Italy, and Germany has been routinely using *torture* or its translation in the headlines over stories on the abuses in the Abu Ghraib prison. And so have the British papers, not just the left-wing *Guardian* ("Torture at Abu Ghraib"), but the right-wing *Express* ("Outrage at U.S. Torture of Prisoners") and even Rupert Murdoch's *Times* ("Inside Baghdad's Torture Jail").

The word *torture* has appeared in the American press, too. Seymour Hersh's story in the *New Yorker* was headed "Torture at Abu Ghraib," and Frank Rich, writing in the *New York Times*, said that Saddam Hussein's torture rooms had been restored to their original use. And a few columnists called the events "atrocities" (a lot more unsettling than simply calling them atrocious).

But most of the American media have been more circum-spect, sticking with vaguer terms like *abuse* and *mistreatment*. Many apparently took their cue from Defense Secretary Rums-feld. Asked about torture in the prison, he said, "What has been charged so far is abuse, which is different from torture. I'm not going to address the 'torture' word."

Others have balked even at talking about *abuse*. In an opin-ion piece in the *Los Angeles Times*, Midge Decter called the treat-ment of detainees a "nasty hazing." Rush Limbaugh said it was "no different than what happens at the Skull and Bones initia-tion. . . . I'm talking about people having a good time. You ever heard of emotional release? You ever heard of need to blow some steam off?" And here in San Francisco, I heard a couple of shock jocks the other day describing the prison as "Abu Grab-Ass" and talking about the treatment in a way that made it sound like *Animal House III: Bluto Bonks Baghdad*.

Some of the reluctance to mention "the 'torture' word" re-flects the effectiveness of the right's campaign against liberal media bias. Journalists or public figures who have ventured to use the word have been taxed with moral equivalence for sug-gesting that the United States was as bad as Saddam.

But a lot of Americans who were genuinely appalled by the photos of the grinning American soldiers had some difficulty connecting them with the words *torture* and *torturer*. Torture may be familiar in the modern world, but it's also remote—we only see it up close in the movies. *Torture* suggests an aes-theticized ritual; it doesn't seem odd that the torture scenes in Gillo Pontecorvo's *Battle of Algiers* should have had a Bach chorale in the background.

In the movies, the torturer's cruelty is invariably counterpoised by a cosmopolitan, effete, and slightly exotic manner—Laurence Olivier in *Marathon Man*, Gert Frobe in *Goldfinger*, or the Mohammed Khan character in *Lives of a Bengal Lancer* telling Gary Cooper, "We have ways of making men talk." Or you think of Vincent Price in almost anything—astringent, urbane, and talking like someone who had lived a lot of his life abroad.

There are no middle-class, middle-American torturers in our gallery, much less torturers with the pudding faces of those GIs, who could have been working at McDonald's a year ago. And the humiliations they were inflicting didn't seem to have much in common with the rituals of pain and submission that *torture* brings to mind. The GIs went down another road, even if it fell off just as sharply.

That's what creates the sense of incongruity we feel when we see those photos. Those may have been far from Delta House high jinks, but you wouldn't know it from the clowning poses the GIs were striking.

In a perverse way, in fact, Decter and Limbaugh may have gotten it right despite themselves. True, *hazing* is a grotesquely dishonest word for this. Leaving aside the severity of the abuses, the prisoners weren't in a position to resign from the fraternity, nor were they about to be given membership pins when pledge week was over. You may as well say that the Los Angeles police were hazing Rodney King.

But what went on in Abu Ghraib has at least this in common with hazing: it's the sort of thing that plenty of ordinary American adolescents with a normal libido might be capable of—or worse, if the circumstances permit. As the Stanford psychologist Phil Zimbardo showed in a famous experiment more than thirty years ago, it doesn't take a lot to transform a group of well-mannered college students into sadistic prison guards, provided someone in authority seems to be giving them the nod.

Not that what the Americans did in Abu Ghraib is really comparable to what went on there during Saddam Hussein's regime, or at least according to what has been made public so far. But it was torture, not just by the definitions of the Geneva Conventions, but by any ordinary standards of decency. Torture is torture is torture, as Secretary Powell put it. If you find yourself having to draw fine semantic distinctions here, you're already way over the line.

And it might be a good idea to acknowledge that torture is not quite as exotic an activity as the movies make it out to be. Looking at the unsettlingly familiar faces of the American soldiers in the Abu Ghraib photos, you realize that what's most disturbing isn't the brutality that is *in*human so much as the brutality that is all too.

ONE FOR FLINCHING

Fresh Air Commentary, October 10, 2006

———

In 1978, the philosopher Henry Shue wrote an influential essay about torture that began: "Whatever one may have to say about torture, there appear to be moral reasons for not saying it." Once we bring the subject up, he asked, mightn't we risk loosening the inhibitions against the whole terrible business? It was easy to have that feeling over the last month or so, as you listened to the country debate just how much cruelty and degradation we were going to allow in interrogating terror suspects. Were we really having this conversation?

In the end, Shue wound up saying that torture had to be talked about—as he put it, "Pandora's Box is already open." But then the topic is irresistible to philosophy professors, since it seems ideally suited to getting students to question their most cherished moral certainties. On the face of things, you'd figure the prohibition of torture would be a top candidate for a categorical moral rule; as the UN convention on torture puts it, there are no exceptional circumstances that justify torture. But what about the scenario of a captured terrorist who has hidden a nuclear bomb that's set to go off in a couple of hours. Would torture be justified then? Some people try to dodge the dilemma by saying that torture never works anyway. But that "never" is a leap of faith—how can you be sure? And anyway, that response leaves the deeper moral question open: Would it be okay to torture the terrorist if you were convinced it *would* get him to tell you where the bomb is? Say no, and you're risking a million lives; say yes, and you've suddenly become a situational relativist, balancing the moral cost of inflicting pain and humiliation against the potential saving of lives.

Most of us find these hypothetical scenarios troubling, as we ought to. But if we're honest, we'll admit that the idea that torture might sometimes be justified can also kindle a prurient thrill. That explains the appeal of the last two seasons of *24*, where episode after episode presents agent Jack Bauer with another opportunity for shooting someone in the kneecap or shocking him with electric wires, always in the interest of getting him to reveal some bit of life-saving information. Whatever your intellectual position on torture, you don't change the channel.

That fascination has deep roots in the folklore of childhood. Who doesn't recall all the ordeals and torture games that children visit on each other? Depending on where or when you grew up, you called them pink belly, the Indian or Chinese rope burn, the noogie or the Russian haircut (aka the Dutch rub)—the names often evoked alien archetypes of cruelty and inhumanity, since even then we knew that Americans didn't do this stuff. But the rituals were compelling even so, a setting for acting out our forbidden fantasies and proving our toughness.

Not surprisingly, the administration was at pains to keep any of that atavistic fascination with torture from bubbling to the surface. We're not suggesting permitting actual *torture*, they insisted—if a terrorist doesn't break under waterboarding or sleep deprivation, we're not going to go all Jack Bauer on him, ticking bomb or no. The challenge was to find language that made the appropriate distinctions: carving the grave breaches of the Geneva Convention from the lesser ones, the stuff that shocks the conscience from the stuff that merely rocks it back on its heels a bit. "Alternative sets of procedures," "enhanced interrogation techniques," "vigorous questioning"—the phrases had a comforting sound of professional routine. In his September 15 speech, in fact, President Bush used the word *professionals* twenty-six times, by way of reassuring Americans that the people administering the procedures would not only know exactly what they were doing but presumably take no pleasure in doing it: "What I'm proposing is that there be clarity in the law so that our professionals will have no doubt that that which they are doing is legal, and so the piece of legislation I sent up there provides our professionals that which is needed to go forward."

Still, some of the administration's supporters were clearly getting a kick out of making light of the procedures under consideration. We're not talking about maiming or killing, they said, and these people have it coming. And anyway, what's the big deal? When the subject of sleep deprivation came up at a House Judiciary Committee hearing last week, Republican Tom Feeney of Florida observed that "there is not an American mom that is guaranteed eight hours of sleep every night." And if playing loud music is inhumane treatment, he added, "virtually every teenager I know is torturing Mom and Dad."

Bill O'Reilly reported that one terrorism suspect had broken when subjected to the music of the Red Hot Chili Peppers, then added, "Well, wouldn't you?" And the *American Spectator*'s Emmett Tyrell argued that waterboarding was infinitely less dangerous than skateboarding, which causes sprained ankles and broken bones.

The point of those comparisons, of course, was to contrast the tough-mindedness of the administration's supporters with the wimpy fastidiousness of its critics—when Colin Powell voiced reservations about the proposals, William F. Buckley called his objections "maudlin." But there was something disturbing about that ostentatious unconcern about what we might be getting ourselves into. There might be a philosophical argument to justify torture in those hypothetical terrorist-with-a-ticking-time-bomb scenarios, though it takes quite a stretch to apply that logic to a Guantanamo suspect picked up in Afghanistan back in 2002. And it's curious that nobody tries to make an argument for legalizing those techniques for police officers interrogating an East LA gangbanger or a Jeffrey Dahmer type, even if you could cook up scenarios for those miscreants that have the same desperate urgency.

But even if you support the use of torture in some cases, it's a conclusion you ought to come to with a sense of gravity and unease, not with belligerent gusto. People have often said that state-approved torture coarsens a society. Actually, to listen to the recent debates, you can achieve that effect just by bringing the subject up. It's striking how eager some people are to embrace their inner school yard bully.

LE TIC, C'EST L'HOMME MÊME

Fresh Air Commentary, July 2, 2004

Which of the major presidential candidates recently began a sentence of a foreign policy speech with the phrase "As complicated as Iraq seems . . . "? You needn't have heard the speech to guess that it was John Kerry—George W. Bush isn't one who's given to pointing out complications. Those differing approaches to complexity have a lot to do with the stylistic contrasts between the two men: the one acknowledging it at every turn, the other gliding over it as if it weren't there.

If you want a key to Kerry's complexity complex, listen to the sentences he begins with *now*. I'm not talking about the *now* that means "at this moment" or the *now* of reproof ("Now that's enough of that"). This is the *now* that announces a reservation or concession, the one that sets up a *but* somewhere down the line—"Now I know it's no beauty, but it will get you to work on time." That's where Kerry piles on his qualifications and hedges before he comes down on a question. Here he is in an interview with the *Washington Post* last month.

Now this administration may have, and I say, may have—I don't
know the answer to this—they also may not have—it may be
that we get Brahimi through a successful process, it may be
there's a sufficient level of deal cut, it may be that the parties
will all quell their individual aspirations long enough to get us
out of there and then reduce the level. I don't know, I mean,
you don't know, either, none of us do. But I'll tell you, we're
not maximizing the potential for the outcome we went in there
to achieve.

That's a typical Kerry comment, with as many forks and
switchbacks as the Boston MTA. The style makes him an easy
mark for charges that he's inconsistent and lacks strong convictions, particularly if you pull out a snippet to use as a sound
bite—"This administration may have. . . . They also may not
have." But Kerry's involuted syntax is less a sign of prevarica-
tion than an excess of prudence. He steps into a thought like
someone wading into a rocky stream, always probing with his
toe for stones. And when he does finally set his foot down, it's
cushioned in abstractions: "We're not maximizing the potential for the outcome we went in there to achieve." When he's
finished, it's not always easy to tell if he has actually touched
bottom.

George Bush rarely allows complexities to cloud his
remarks—even if he wanted to, his syntax wouldn't be up to
it. In fact he often conveys a puzzlement that things aren't as
clear to others as they are to him. You can hear that attitude in
his predilection for beginning sentences with *see* or *you see*,
which he'll sometimes do half a dozen times in a single press
conference. Ordinarily, you use those expressions when you're

letting your listeners in on a hidden explanation, something you know that they don't: "See, that's why they wrap them that way, so you can't tell they've shrunk the package." But the remarks that Bush begins with *see* are rarely things that would come as news to the audience—they're more often platitudes, truisms, or familiar bits of conservative dogma:

> This economy of ours is strengthening, and that's positive. See, we want people working here in America.
>
> They know there is no future for them in a free society. You see, they're trying to shake our will.
>
> [This conflict] has come to us by the choices of violent men, hateful men. See, we seek peace.

When Bush is on a roll, he'll stick in two or three of these *sees* in a row, as he did in addressing the American Conservative Union on May 13: "We want younger workers to own and manage their own retirement accounts. See, we understand, when people have assets to call their own, they gain independence and security and dignity. See, I believe in private property so much, I want every American to have some."

It isn't likely Bush thought that any of those remarks introduced by *see* would strike his audience as revelations—but then that isn't really what he's doing with the word. It's like beginning a sentence with "Let me tell you a little secret" or "This may come as news to you, but . . ."—a way of packaging a truism as if it were inside information, with the implication that there are some people who may not find it as obvious as you and I do. It's as if to say that the world is really a simple place, except to the people who make things too complicated to see the truth in front of their noses. "See, I believe you have to ask for the vote." "See, terrorists hate freedom."

To Bush's supporters, that little habit conveys resolute self-confidence. But others are apt to hear it as smug and simplistic, the same way that Kerry's elaborate verbal hedging can make him sound overcomplicated and equivocal. That may seem a lot to lay on the back of a few conversational tics, but then sometimes the prefatory noises we make unconsciously can be more revealing than the words that follow them. "The style is the man himself," said the Count de Buffon in the eighteenth century. People sometimes quote that dictum as if it meant that a man was no more than his style. But Buffon wasn't being reductive. He meant only that there's no choice we make that doesn't open a little window on our nature.

MODERATE TO A FAULT

Fresh Air Commentary, September 1, 2004

———

By their uniforms you shall know them. *The New York Times'* Damien Cave begins an article on the Republican convention by saying, "They are finally here: the Republican delegates with their rep ties." Daniel Peres, the editor of *Details* magazine, explains why he's leaving the city for the duration: "I don't want to see a lot of bad Men's Warehouse suits and a lot of badly parted hair walking around my neighborhood." *New York* magazine offers tips to women conventioneers on where to buy coordinated skirt suits and high-end hair spray. And the *Weekly Standard's* Mark Labash worries that in New York, Republicans will stand out like Good Humor men in their summer-weight khaki suits.

Unfair or not, those stereotypes have a long history. *White-shoes Republicans* goes back to the Reagan years. And then of course there's the "Checkers" speech that Richard Nixon gave during the 1952 campaign, with its famous reference to "respectable Republican cloth coat." What's curious is that people weren't pigeonholing the Democrats that way when they gathered for their conclave in Boston last month. Liberals, yes, with their Volvos, lattes, and Birkenstocks. But the Democratic Party in general gets a sartorial pass.

The picture of a Republican uniform mirrors a wider perception of the party's ideological uniformity. It's a difference that shows up in the words we use to describe the parties. When the Republicans wanted to put a compassionate face on their party for the convention, they decided to feature speakers like Rudy Giuliani, Arnold Schwarzenegger, George Pataki, and Michael Bloomberg. That pretty much mirrors the strategy the Democrats adopted at their convention when they tried to appeal to swing voters with speakers like Senator John Breaux of Louisiana and Barack Obama of Illinois. The difference is that the Republican speakers tend to be called moderates, whereas the Democrats are called centrists.

In fact, when politicians are described as centrists, the odds are around 4 to 1 they're Democrats. When they're described as moderates, the odds are 4 to 1 they're Republicans. People tend to place Democrats relative to the broad political spectrum and Republicans relative to their party. In press stories, for example, *mainstream Republican* is three times more common than *mainstream Democrat* is.*

Those discrepancies are a fairly recent development. *Moderate* has been around for a long time to describe liberals or conservatives who are "not rootin'-tootin'," as William Safire has put it. But the phrase *moderate Republican* didn't become com-

---

*There was a time when *left-wing* and *right-wing* were relative terms, as well. Back in 1958, the *Chicago Tribune* could describe Senators Jacob Javits, Hugh Scott, and George W. Bush's grandfather Prescott Bush as "Republican leftists" without any implication that they were infected with socialistic views.

mon until the 1964 election. At the time, it implied a contrast with the "extremist" label that was being pinned on Barry Goldwater and his supporters—Nelson Rockefeller used the description in an effort to peel off conservative Republicans who were unsympathetic to the liberal label but who might also have qualms about Goldwater. But the phrase persisted even after conservative Republicanism became respectable in the Reagan era. When Tom DeLay jokes about how many moderates the Republican Party has, he obviously isn't contrasting moderates with radicals or extremists. Nowadays, being a moderate Republican is usually a matter of what position you take on social issues, or sometimes just a matter of tone. Moderate Republicans are like other Republicans, only more affable about it.

The triumph of *moderate Republican* owes a lot to the near disappearance of the phrase *liberal Republican*, which is less than a quarter as common in the press than it was in Goldwater's day. That's partly a consequence of the party's general drift to the right. But the fact is that a lot of the speakers who are featured at the convention would probably have been called liberal Republicans in the 1960s.

Since then, though, the polarization of political life has been turning the l-word into an absolute rather than a relative term. Nowadays Republicans like Pataki and Bloomberg wouldn't own up to being a liberal anything, no more than they'd acknowledge Nelson Rockefeller or John Lindsay as their spiritual ancestors.

Ever since the Reagan years, we've been describing the two parties with different sets of coordinates. We define Republicans by their positions in the party constellation; we define

Democrats according to their distance from the absolute political horizons. That reflects the view of Republicans as having a dominant ideology, which defines the party's center and
periphery. We have a word *Republicanism*, after all, but there's
no word *Democratism*.

For that matter, Republicans are much more likely than Democrats to be described as *true believers* or as the *party faithful*.
The language suggests that the Republicans are a movement,
whereas the Democrats are a confluence of currents with no
discernable mainstream. As Will Rogers famously said, "I belong to no organized party—I'm a Democrat."

This isn't to say that people don't perceive the Democrats as
standing for anything nowadays. Compassionate conservatism
or no, words like *caring* and *fairness* are still more likely to come
up in connection with Democrats. But that's a question of
common attitudes and values rather than of a political program. Despite all the efforts of the right to make *Democrat* syn-
onymous with *liberal*, people don't associate the party with a
dominant philosophical system.

Those differences are natural, given the Republicans' fabled
party discipline and the Democrats' equally fabled fractious-
ness, compounded by all those years out of power. But the perception of the Republicans' overriding ideological unity may
make it hard to persuade undecided voters that people like
Bloomberg and Schwarzenegger are the real embodiments of
the party's soul. Not with all those qualifying adjectives slung
around their necks—and certainly not in those fabulous suits.

EVEN IN ENGLISH IT'S HARD TO TRANSLATE

Los Angeles Times, October 14, 2004

The genius of language is to comprehend different things under a single name, but that's also what can make it deceptive. Most of the proposals that President Bush has been touting to restructure taxes have been floating around for quite a while— offering tax incentives for establishing health savings accounts, reducing taxes on investment income, and allowing workers to redirect some of their payroll taxes into investment accounts. But even critics of these programs acknowledge that they acquire a new appeal to Americans when bundled as part of *the ownership society.*

But for all the slogan's domestic allure, the foreign press has had a hard time explaining it. The Italian daily *La Stampa* rendered the phrase as the *società dei proprietari,* or "society of property owners." The German edition of the *Financial Times* used *Teilhabergesellschaft,* or "shareholder society." And a writer for the French business journal *Les Echos* rendered the phrase as *la société de la proprieté,* using a word that can mean either "property" or "legal ownership," but added that the English word *ownership* is so vague that the phrase is basically untranslatable.

Foreigners have the same problem with Bush's description of the programs as "empowering people to help themselves." The best the Finns can do to render *empowerment* is a phrase that means "being in charge of one's life." The French sometimes paraphrase it as "emancipation" or "active participation," but usually they just leave it in English and hope for the best.

And although German has a word that literally means "empowerment," it trails some awkward historical connotations. The *Ermächtigungsgesetz*, or Empowerment Act, was the 1933 law that allowed Adolf Hitler to rule by decree—one reason why the Germans too usually opt for the English word.

Of course there are plenty of other English words—such as *cozy* and *smug*—that resist translation. But when foreigners are scratching their heads over the keywords of our political debates, it's usually a sign that somebody is trying to get away with some semantic sleight of hand.

The Europeans' puzzlement over *ownership society* doesn't reflect an obstinately collectivist mentality. They don't have any trouble expressing the idea of owning a house, a bistro, or a hundred shares of stock. But they're mystified when we talk about people owning things in ways detached from legal possession.

Self-help gurus talk about "owning your feelings" (presumably preferable to renting). Business consultants stress the importance of getting employees to "feel ownership," not by giving them an equity stake but by encouraging them to "celebrate the company's vision." Nowadays, pride of ownership doesn't always require a deed.

That psychological sense of ownership is always in the background when Bush and others talk about ownership as an abstract social good. "In a new term," he says, "we'll continue to spread ownership to every corner of America." On its face, that sounds a lot like Oprah's "Everybody gets a car!" But Bush's *ownership* is a lot broader and vaguer than that—it simultaneously promises an increase in wealth, individual responsibility, and personal control.

There's no question that enabling people to acquire property and assets gives them a sense of control of their lives and of having a stake in society. In that sense, an ownership society is everybody's dream. That's why liberals have stressed the importance of redressing disparities in personal wealth and of reversing the alarming drop in net worth of the bottom 40 percent of the US population.

But critics have charged that Bush's proposals would actually increase those disparities, by displacing the tax burden from investment income to wages and by favoring those in the top brackets who naturally benefit most from tax incentives. From that point of view, Bush's *owners* can seem just an oblique synonym for *haves*.

The problem with big-tent words like *ownership* is that they obscure the discord among their meanings; it can take a while to realize that one sense of ownership can work at cross-purposes to another. Younger workers may derive a psychological satisfaction from controlling their own retirement accounts; as investors, we all like to think we're a bit smarter than average. But if these workers make the wrong choices, they could wind up owning less and might ruefully recall why it was called social security in the first place.

But *the ownership society* deftly obscures those trade-offs, conflating personal control and financial well-being. In the midst of an electoral campaign, Republicans aren't about to point out that ownership can come down to saying you're on your own.

THE BOOK OF SAMUELS

Fresh Air Commentary, November 29, 2005

In an age when public discussion about the language is relegated to Sunday supplement features and the perky titles in the language corner at the back of the bookstore, it's hard for us to understand why Samuel Johnson's *Dictionary of the English Language* had such political importance when it was first published 250 years ago.

The *Dictionary* appeared at a moment of intense anxiety about the language. Britain had only just become what Johnson called "a nation of readers," as public opinion, shaped by the press and print literature, was challenging the authority of traditional institutions like the monarchy, the church, and Parliament. But how could you count on printed words to determine social values when they seemed to change their meanings from one speaker to another or from one generation to the next? As William Warburton wrote in the preface to his 1747 edition of Shakespeare: "We have neither Grammar nor Dictionary, neither Chart nor Compass, to guide us through this wide sea of Words."

Johnson's wasn't the first English dictionary, but it spoke with an obvious authority that allayed many of those anxieties. It seemed to capture the elusive and fluttering meanings of words and pin their wings to its pages. "As the weight of truth and reason is irresistible," Robert Nares wrote of the *Dictionary* in 1784, "its authority has nearly fixed the external form of our language; and from its decisions few appeals have yet been made." That was overoptimistic. Johnson included numerous words that would soon vanish, like *ariolation* ("soothsaying") and *clancular* ("clandestine"), while objecting to items like *budge, cajole,* and *job,* which eventually became standard English.

In any event, the dictionary's role in settling meanings has always been symbolic more than actual. True, a concise definition can pin down the basic meaning of a concrete word like *marlinspike, margrave,* or *marmoreal.* But we don't really expect a dictionary to delineate the finer nuances of more abstract words, particularly the ones that are charged with social or political importance. A college freshman can begin a composition on terrorism or suicide with "According to Merriam-Webster's dictionary," but you wouldn't take seriously an essay in the *Atlantic* or the *New Republic* that opened with the same formula. Nobody really expects that you can do justice to a complex concept in a five- or ten-word definition whose parts are themselves subject to dispute—it's like trying to use an AAA street map to resolve a dispute with your neighbor over your lot lines.

For most of its existence, in fact, the Supreme Court rarely referred to dictionaries to determine the meanings of the statutes it was considering. Justices Holmes, Brandeis, and Cardozo didn't once cite a dictionary in all their years on the court.

It's only in recent years that the use of dictionaries has become a routine practice. Since 1990, the Court has referred to dictionary definitions in more cases than in the preceding two centuries of its life.

You can attribute that to the rise of the legal doctrine of textualism. When courts are trying to determine the meaning of a statute or regulation, the doctrine says, they should look only at the plain meanings of the words of the text itself, not the intentions of Congress or the legislative history of the law. And where better to look than in the neutral source that most people turn to when they want to settle a dispute over meaning?

So it's not surprising that the justice who has referred to dictionaries most often is Antonin Scalia, the most eloquent advocate of textualism, followed by Clarence Thomas—though to judge from Samuel Alito's penchant for citing dictionaries in his decisions, he might give both of them a run for their money.

But using a dictionary to determine the meanings of words turns out to be not quite the objective procedure that most of us take it to be. Some dictionaries define words more broadly than others. And when a dictionary gives several meanings for a word, judges have a lot of discretion in deciding which of them is most appropriate.

Judicial restraint or no, dictionaries give courts a lot of wiggle room. It's no wonder the Court's debates about the meanings of words can resemble food fights among unruly children, in the words of Brooklyn Law School professor Lawrence Solan.

In one 1993 case, the Supreme Court ruled that a man who traded a rifle for some cocaine could be sentenced under a statute that provided for an increased penalty for someone who uses a firearm to obtain narcotics. Writing for the majority, Justice O'Connor justified the decision by citing one dictionary's definition of *use* as "to employ." To his credit, Justice Scalia dissented, following a principle of interpretation that you could paraphrase as "give me a break, please." In ordinary usage, he said, using a firearm means using it as a weapon, not as a medium of barter.

But Scalia himself hasn't been above what the legal scholar Ellen Aprill calls "dictionary shopping." Does the word *representatives* as used in the 1982 Voting Rights Act apply to elected judges in addition to legislators? In a 1991 decision, Scalia said it didn't. He cited the definition of the word in the 1934 Webster's *Second International*—a dictionary that some language traditionalists regard with the kind of reverence that folk purists have for Bob Dylan's acoustic era. But if he'd wanted to argue the other way, he could have referred to the broader definitions of *representative* in the more recent Webster's *Third* or the *American Heritage*, both of which he has found it convenient to cite on other occasions.

But the most dramatic recent example of the selective use of dictionaries comes not from a Supreme Court decision but from the memorandum on torture that was written for the Justice Department in 2002 by Assistant Attorney General Jay S. Bybee, who has since been appointed to the Ninth Circuit Court of Appeals. By cherry-picking his dictionaries and senses, Bybee managed to come up with a definition of *torture* that ruled out any practice that doesn't cause lasting impairment or inflict pain that rises to the level of death or organ damage. By that standard, nothing that happened at Abu Ghraib would count as torture, even if most people would describe it that way. It's a far cry from the plain meaning of the word, but the appeal to a dictionary seems to cloak the definition in Johnsonian disinterestedness.

Johnson himself approached his project with more humility. He wrote that no dictionary could reduce to mechanical certainty "the boundless chaos of a living speech." There's no greater slight to his memory than to pretend now that that's a done deal.

TOUCHY, AREN'T WE?

Fresh Air Commentary, June 29, 2006

═══════

It may be hard to believe when you listen to the ambient chatter, but contemporary public discourse is actually no more rancorous than it was in ages past. As Eric Burns notes in his new book *Infamous Scribblers* the American press was malicious and mendacious from the outset, and by most historical standards the tone of our present dialogue is positively genteel.

What's novel is the tone and setting of the chatter. Americans have always enjoyed the spectacle of political brouhahas, but before the advent of talk radio and Fox News, nobody realized that you could build a successful business model on political invective all by itself. If you care to, you can hear more political name-calling in a single week than Americans of earlier eras could experience in an entire lifetime. Political chatter has become a form of performance art, as artificial and formulaic as reality TV.

Take Ann Coulter's recent description of the 9/11 widows as self-obsessed witches who were enjoying their husbands' deaths. As calumnies go, it doesn't have a patch on the things people were saying in the 1864 election, when the Democrats called Lincoln a leering buffoon and Horace Greeley accused the Democrats of stealing the votes of dead Union soldiers. But it's only in the current age that remarks like those could turn someone into a media celebrity who's invited to appear on *Jay Leno* and the *Today Show* to repeat her choicest remarks for the delectation or outrage of their viewers.

Coulter's celebrity is a good indication of what has become of political discussion. You'd scarcely describe her as a political thinker, no more than you'd describe Simon Cowell as a critic of the arts. But like Cowell, she has a unerring instinct for media theatrics. It isn't just her penchant for making snarky or outrageous remarks. Plenty of people do that without being invited onto the *Today Show*, and in fact Coulter doesn't get a lot of national attention for her run-of-the-mill ruminations about giving rat poison to Justice Stevens or fragging John Murtha. But the remark about the 9/11 widows was irresistible for its brazen and gratuitous tastelessness and the obvious pleasure Coulter took in the consternation she created.

Is Coulter sincere about the things she says? That's a silly question, like asking whether schoolchildren are sincere in the taunts they throw at each other across the school yard. But that doesn't make her a satirist, as her defenders like to claim, usually with the implication that her literal-minded liberal critics don't get the joke.

Satire depicts things as grotesque to make them seem ridiculous—what Stephen Colbert does in his Bill O'Reilly persona or Christopher Buckley does with the pointed caricatures of *Thank You for Smoking*. But Coulter isn't actually sending anybody up—not herself, certainly, and not the targets of her remarks. Her fans may enjoy hearing her talk about poisoning Justice Stevens or say that it's a pity Timothy McVeigh didn't park his truck next to the *New York Times*' building. But that's not because the remarks make either Stevens or the *New York Times* seem particularly ridiculous. It's because Coulter seems to be able to get away with unbridled aggression by presenting it as mere mischief, leaving her critics looking prim and humorless. "Perhaps her book should have been called 'Heartless,'" said Hillary Clinton after Coulter's remarks about the widows, inviting the response, "Oh lighten *up*, girl."

That rhetorical maneuver doesn't have a name of its own, but you could think of it as a form of smut. In the strict sense, as Freud said in *Jokes and Their Relation to the Unconscious,* smut is the verbal gesture that replaces overt sexual aggression, like the leering innuendo the men at the tavern aim at the barmaid. But in a looser sense, smut could be any kind of malicious aggression that pretends to be mere naughtiness. It might be a leering vulgarity, a racial epithet, or simply a venomous insult—what makes it smut is that it's tricked out as humor, so that if anyone claims to be offended, you can answer indignantly, "Can't you take a joke?"

In that broad sense, smut can sometimes be innocuous fun. It's a staple of sitcoms, in what you could think of as a "Woooo!" moment. That's the moment when a character who's comically malicious or catty (think Betty White, Rhea Perlman, Joseph Marcell) makes a remark that's just offensive or risqué enough to brush the limits of taste, and the studio audience reacts by saying, "Woooo!"

The political talk shows traffic in these moments, too—not surprising, considering how much those shows owe to the clas-

sic sitcom. When you think of the most successful practitioners of the genre, whether Coulter, O'Reilly, or James Carville,
there isn't a one of them who couldn't be the model for a recurring character on *Cheers* or *Drew Carey*—the waspish virago,
the bombastic blowhard, the sly yokel.

And as on the sitcoms, the drama of the political talk show
is character-driven rather than plot-driven. Watching O'Reilly
or Hannity and Colmes, you can't help recalling the bickering
on *All in the Family*, where politics was always just a pretext for
the clash of personalities. It doesn't matter whether the ostensible issue is the massacre at Haditha or a spike in wild bache-
lorette parties; it's going to be reduced to grist for the eternal
squabble between liberals and conservatives—not as adherents
of opposing political philosophies, but more as distinct political genders. ("Who are these parents who allow their kids to
sleep with Michael Jackson?" Alan Colmes asked a couple of
years back, and Sean Hannity answered, "Liberals.")

It's that underlying comic framework that creates the opportunity for political smut. However rude or offensive a remark might sound in the abstract, it's all in the spirit of fun,
isn't it? And as Coulter and other adepts of the genre understand, the ultimate effect is to aggravate the affront, not alle-
viate it. You not only get to offer an insult, but get to discredit
the anger or outrage it evokes as prim political correctness:
"My, we're touchy, aren't we?"

That's the singular rhetorical achievement of our age. Other
periods may have been our equals at mere abuse, but no one
can touch us when it comes to driving people up a wall.

PROGRESSIVE TO A FAULT

Fresh Air Commentary, October 27, 2006

═══════════

People don't like distinctions without differences. Soda and pop, rap and hip hop, breakfast nooks and dinettes—however close two words seem to be, we're going to try to tease out a difference in meaning.

So as more people take to styling themselves as "progressives" rather than "liberals," it isn't surprising to see efforts to carve out an ideological difference between the two labels. At the *New Republic*'s academic blog, the historian Eric Rauchway traces the origins of the distinction to the Roosevelt era, when the early twentieth-century progressive movement was giving way to the liberalism of the New Deal. The difference, he says, is that liberals are content to make an uneasy truce with capitalism, while progressives favor more vigorous social experimentation. And the political writer David Sirota argues that liberals favor expanded social programs whereas progressives favor more direct limitations on corporate power.

Those are principled philosophical distinctions, and so are many of the others that people have proposed. But none of them has much to do with how the labels are actually used. You can't predict how people will describe themselves by polling them on the issues or interviewing them about their philosophy of government. And for that matter, you don't really have to. You have a pretty good idea which people are going to call themselves progressives without knowing how they come down on single-payer health care. It's more informative to know that they live in a university town or work for a non-profit, listen to Pacifica radio rather than NPR, read blogs like Daily Kos and Eschaton, and wouldn't share a summer rental with anybody who voted for George Bush.

That all has less to do with ideology than genealogy. Far more than liberals, progressives see themselves in the line of the historical left. Not that America has much of a left to speak of anymore, at least by the standards of the leftists of the Vietnam era, who were a lot less eager than most modern-day progressives to identify themselves with the Democratic Party. But if modern progressives haven't inherited the radicalism or ferocity of the movement left of the '60s, they're doing what they can to keep its tone and attitude alive.

At the heart of that attitude was a sense of superiority to all those middle-class liberals whose wan political commitments were tempered by self-interest. In 1962, Norman Mailer wrote, "I don't care if people call me a radical, a rebel, a red, a revolutionary, an outsider, an outlaw, a Bolshevik, an anarchist, a nihilist, or even a left conservative, but please don't ever call me a liberal." A couple of years later, Phil Ochs sang "Love Me, I'm a Liberal," a sarcastic catalogue of the hypocrisies of middle-class liberals:

> I go to all the Pete Seeger concerts
> He sure gets me singing those songs,
> I'll send all the money you ask for,
> But don't ask me to come on along.
> So love me, love me, love me, I'm a liberal.

When Ochs wrote those words, of course, the liberal label was still riding high in the saddle. In 1961, the philosopher Charles Frankel observed that "anyone who today identifies himself as an unmitigated opponent of liberalism . . . cannot aspire to influence on the national political scene." Little more than a decade later, the label was in tatters, the victim of the sharp divisions over Vietnam, the backlash against civil rights, and the perceived failure of the Great Society social programs. That was when the right began to color liberals with new social stereotypes, fitting them out with Volvos, white wine, brie, and other accoutrements that suggested their vast distance from heartland Middle Americans.

By the 1980s, Democratic politicians were cutting and running from the liberal label, particularly after Ronald Reagan branded it as "the L-Word" in a speech to the 1988 Republican convention. Some of them explained their reluctance to use the label as part of a general aversion to pigeonholing: when you hear a politician say, "I don't believe in labels," you can be pretty sure you're listening to someone who would have proudly worn the liberal label forty years ago.

But others switched over to the progressive label, so as not to evoke any of those fatuous L-Word stereotypes. Often, in fact, the label has had no particular ideological significance at all. The Progressive Policy Institute was established in 1989 to develop a centrist "Third Way" program for the Democrats. And during the 2003 California recall election, Gray Davis contrasted Arnold Schwarzenegger's "conservative agenda" with his own "progressive agenda"—this from a Democrat who had never been known for cruising in the party's left lane. It's the same strategy that the Ford Motor Company adopted after the Edsel bombed in the late 1950s—they changed the grille and trim and successfully marketed it as the Ford Galaxie, in the hope that nobody would notice it was the same car.

When Berkeley professors or social activists use the progressive label among themselves, it's the political equivalent of a fraternity handshake—*they* know that it's meant to convey their ideological purity, rather than simply to downplay their Volvo ownership. But those nuances are apt to be lost on Americans who have no idea that the word *Progressive* ever wore a capital letter—people who not only haven't heard of Walter Lippmann or Robert Lafollette but are probably a little cloudy on Phil Ochs, too. For them, the P-Word is simply a way of avoiding saying the L-Word, which is the term everybody else uses for the left-hand pole of American politics, etched on the split screens of the cable talk shows. It seems to confirm the suspicion that liberals don't talk the same language as other Americans, even when it comes to pronouncing their own name right.

That's the progressives' bind: you can't distance yourself from the negative liberal stereotypes of Phil Ochs without also corroborating the negative liberal stereotypes of Rush Limbaugh. The more Democrats avoid the liberal label, the more cheerfully the right steps in to redefine it, driving it to the margins of political life. (Not long ago, the Republican minority leader of the South Carolina Senate described a Democratic legislator as "one of the most liberal leftists that we have in the House"—a description that would have sounded dyslexic thirty years ago.)

Of course progressives will tell you in all sincerity that they're not out to trash the liberal label and insist that their differences with liberals are fundamentally philosophical, not stylistic, even if it isn't easy to put your finger on what they are. The irony is that nowadays it's often that insistence alone that divides the two. The main difference between progressives and liberals is that progressives believe that there is one.

ISLAMO-CREEPS WOULD BE MORE ACCURATE

Los Angeles Times, September 17, 2006

———

It wasn't the first time President Bush had described the United States as at war with "Islamic fascists." But coming in his remarks about the arrests of two dozen terror suspects in Britain last week, the phrase signaled that the administration was shopping for new language to defend its policies at a time when the evocations of the "war on terror" don't seem to stem rising doubts about the wisdom of "staying the course" in Iraq.

Hence the appeal of using *Islamo-fascism*, as people often call it, which links the current conflict to images from the last just war: Nazi tanks rolling into Poland and France, spineless collaborators sapping the national will, Winston Churchill glaring defiantly over his cigar, the black ink spreading across the maps of Europe and Asia in the *Why We Fight* propaganda documentaries that Frank Capra made for the US Army Signal Corps.

Squint in just the right way, and the parallels are easy to see. In a speech at the National Press Club last month, GOP Senator Rick Santorum of Pennsylvania raised the specter of the

Islamists' dreams of "a new, global caliphate where Islamic fascism will rule mankind" and reminded the audience that "we had no problem understanding that Nazism and fascism were evil racist empires. We must now bring the same clarity to the war against Islamic fascism."

In that picture of things, everything is connected: last week's arrests in London and Birmingham are linked to the Iraq occupation as closely as the London blitz was to Stalingrad during the last great anti-fascist struggle. Those were the connections Vice President Dick Cheney was presuming when he said that Ned Lamont's victory over Joe Lieberman in the Connecticut Democratic primary would embolden the "Al Qaeda types" who are trying to "break the will of the American people."

The phrase *Islamo-fascism* has been around for more than fifteen years. But it was only after 9/11 that neocons and other hard-liners seized on it to justify a broad-based military campaign against Islamic governments and groups hostile to the West.

If you take it at face value, *Islamo-fascism* doesn't make a lot of sense. The "fascist" part might fit Saddam Hussein's Iraq, with its militaristic nationalism, its secret police, and its silly peaked officers' hats. But there was nothing "Islamo-" about the regime; Iraq's Baathists tried to make the state the real object of the people's devotion.

That's why it's odd to describe repressive theocracies like the Taliban as fascist—just as it would be for Savonarola's Florence, John Calvin's Geneva, or the Spain of the Inquisition, all of which reduced the state to an instrument for enforcing God's will. The Islamic world doesn't seem to offer very fertile soil for fascist cults of the state. In a 2005 Pew Global Attitudes survey, large majorities in most Muslim nations said their loyalty to Islam came before their loyalty as citizens.

But in the mouths of the neocons, *fascist* is just an evocative label for people who are fanatical, violent, and anti-democratic. In fact, the word is no more precise for them than it was for the 1960s radicals who used it as a one-size-fits-all epithet for the Nixon administration, American capitalism, the police, reserved concert seating, and all other varieties of social control that disinclined them to work on Maggie's farm no more.

Back then, conservatives derided the left for using *fascism* so promiscuously. They didn't discover the usefulness of the elastic f-word until the fall of communism left traditional right-wing slurs such as *communistic* and *pinko* sounding quaint.

Time was when right-wingers called the ACLU a bunch of communist sympathizers. Now Bill O'Reilly labels the group and others as fascist, with a cavalier disregard for semantic niceties that would have done the Weathermen proud. But then, it's the point of symbolic words such as *fascist* to ease the burden of thought—as Walter Lippmann observed, they "assemble emotions after they've been detached from their ideas." And it may be that Americans are particularly vulnerable to using *fascism* sloppily, never having experienced the real thing close up.

But like *terror,* and *evil* before it, *Islamic fascism* has the effect of reducing a complex story to a simple fable. It effaces the differences among ex-Baathists, Al Qaeda, and Shiite mullahs; Chechens and Kashmiris; Hezbollah, Hamas, and British-born Asians making bombs in a London suburb. Yes, there are millions of people in the Muslim world who wish the United States ill, and some of them are pretty creepy about it. But that doesn't mean they're all of a single mind and purpose, or that a blow against any one of them is a blow against the others. As Tolstoy might have put it, every creep is creepy in his own way.

WARS AND WORD GAMES

Los Angeles Times, December 3, 2006

━━━━━━

In 1781, the American patriot James Duane denounced the British government for describing the fighting in the American colonies as a rebellion rather than a civil war. "Rebellion," Duane said, "is only applied to such Insurrection as is void of all Appearance of Justice." But when the sovereign's opponents "have some Reason for Taking arms" and become so strong that he "finds himself Compelled to make war regularly on them, he must be contented with the Term of Civil War"— and hence, Duane added, must treat his adversaries as legitimate combatants.

Two centuries later, those are pretty much the same implications that the Bush administration has been resisting when it refuses to use *civil war* to describe the situation in Iraq. The term doesn't simply underscore the Iraqi government's inability to check the warring factions, leaving US forces caught in the middle. It also implies the need for a shift in policy. People think of insurgencies and insurrections as things that can be suppressed or defeated, but when it comes to civil wars, prudence usually calls for stepping smartly out of the line of fire and seeking a political solution.

For many, to talk about a civil war in Iraq is simply to "face the reality," as Colin Powell said last week in explaining why he was using the term. The *Los Angeles Times* has been using the phrase since early October, and it has since been adopted by *NBC News* as the appropriate term for "armed militarized factions fighting for their own political agendas." That's similar to the working definition of a civil war that political scientists often use: an internal military conflict that results in more than a thousand battle deaths a year—which would put Iraq well over the threshold.

But the administration and its supporters have been more exacting in their definitions. The Iraq situation is not a civil war, said White House Press Secretary Tony Snow, but merely "sectarian violence that seems to be less aimed at gaining full control over an area than expressing differences." And British military historian Sir John Keegan argues that a civil war requires not only that both sides have recognized leaders and clear political agendas but that uniformed armies meet on a field of battle—a definition that fits only five conflicts over the last two hundred years and one that would ensure that, however out-of-hand things get, Iraq will almost certainly be spared a true civil war.

But the English language doesn't owe scholars a living. Nothing magical happens when an insurrection exacts its thousandth casualty or when the sides don uniforms. Nor has history reserved *civil war* for conflicts with two clearly defined sides. As Duane observed more than two hundred years ago, that's simply the term we use when groups with political agendas can wage protracted campaigns against the government.

Politicians who want to avoid using terms with inopportune implications invariably maintain that their choice of words is guided by their concern for semantic exactitude rather than a desire to manage impressions. *Recession, genocide*—the political lexicon is full of terms with reassuringly strict, official definitions, even if they're actually no more amenable to neat characterization than *bad hair day*. Or think of all the efforts to define *torture* in a way that exempts "enhanced interrogation techniques," as the CIA calls them. "We do not torture," President Bush has said, and in the interest of preserving that principle, the administration has formulated elaborately precise criteria to distinguish the inhuman from the merely regrettable.

But in the end, it's history that determines what counts as what, not governments. And as it happens, history defines civil wars not just by who's fighting and why, but by how the struggle comes out. We usually don't remember conflicts as civil wars if the state isn't intact when the smoke has cleared.

A few months after Duane wrote his remarks, for example, George Washington and the Marquis de Lafayette defeated Lord Cornwallis at Yorktown, ensuring that history would record the conflict as neither rebellion nor civil war but a war of independence. For that matter, it's unlikely we would still be speaking of the American Civil War if Pickett's Charge had succeeded in breaking the Union lines at Gettysburg.

More recently, people ceased talking about a civil war in Yugoslavia once it became clear that "Yugoslavia" itself had become a historical irrelevancy. No one can say whether Iraq will suffer the same fate. But acknowledging that what's going on is in fact a civil war—and dealing with it accordingly—would be one step toward making sure that history will remember it as one, rather than simply as the conflagration that ultimately broke the country apart.

CHUMP CHANGE

Fresh Air Commentary, January 14, 2008

═══════

The most incisive summary I've seen of the current electoral rhetoric was an editorial cartoon by Matt Davies that appeared in last week's LA *Times*. A man is walking his dog past a lawn bristling with signs that read "Huckabee for change," "Edwards for Change," "Obama Change," "Romney says change in '08," and so forth, as he thinks to himself, "Same ol', same ol'."

Well, yes and no. It doesn't take a lot of political savvy to trot out the c-word when the administration and Congress are unpopular, the economy is in free fall, and three-quarters of the electorate say that the country is on the wrong track. Change has always been the obvious card for nonincumbents to play, whatever direction they're planning to head in. When he first ran for president in 1992, Bill Clinton described himself as "the change we need." Jimmy Carter billed himself in 1976 as "a leader for a change," which voters were free to take as a dig at Gerald Ford. In 1952, after twenty years of Democratic rule, the Republicans campaigned for Eisenhower under the official slogan "It's time for a change," though they used the snappier "I like Ike" for jingles and campaign buttons.

But the language of change itself has changed in the interim. In 1952, Eisenhower would never have thought to describe himself as a "change agent," which to most people would have conjured up nothing more than a guy passing out coins at a booth in the subway. Back then, *change agent* was still an obscure bit of social-science jargon for an innovator or what people now call an *early adapter*—the first villager to buy a bicycle, the first doctor to try a new procedure.

By the 1980s *change agent* was showing up in corporate jargon with a somewhat grander meaning, as the trait that separates the managerial mice and men. At least that's how the story is told by the motivational writer Spencer Johnson in his best-selling *Who Moved My Cheese?* The work is a ninety-four-page fable set in a maze inhabited by two mice and by two little humans named Hem and Haw, who discover one day that their daily ration of cheese is not in its customary place. They whine and curse their fate until Haw realizes that they have to overcome their debilitating fear of change and boldly resolve to seek out new cheese elsewhere.

Who Moved My Cheese? has been a huge success with managers, who don't seem to see anything condescending in an allegory that depicts workers as creatures scurrying for cheese in a maze. Since its publication in 1998 it has sold more than 5 million copies, including carloads shipped to companies like Southwest Airlines and General Motors for distribution to their employees.

Of course employees are apt to be apprehensive when copies of the book start to show up in their mailboxes, since they know that the change they're about to be encouraged to embrace will likely come not in the abstract, but in the form of a plural noun—as in "We're going to be making some changes around here." That's not a sentence most people are happy to hear these days, particularly if they happen to be working for an airline or automobile company.

Still, the label *change agent* has the heroic ring of other new corporate job descriptions like *champion, road warrior,* and *thought leader.* In an age that has turned CEOs into media icons, it suggests that business success is a validation of personal charisma, not simply competence. And modern managers are naturally gratified by the suggestion that the challenge of constant change is more urgent and daunting for them than it was in the leisurely days when Alfred P. Sloan was running General Motors and FDR was running the country.

It was inevitable that the term would show up in politics, as both Republicans and Democrats took to talking about government with the language of business, so that every education or public health program had to be justified as an "investment in human capital." In fact it isn't surprising that the New Democrat Bill Clinton would become the first national politician to describe himself as a change agent when he launched his run for the presidency in 1991, at another moment of voter discontent with the economy and the government. In the current campaign nearly every candidate has claimed the change agent label, and last week Bill Clinton upped the ante when he described Hillary Clinton as a "world-class change agent." Fifty years from now, that phrase will be as evocative of the Clinton era as "23 skidoo" is of the age of Warren Harding.

Any label as accommodating as *change agent* is going to be wholly empty of substance. It's a statement about your personality, not your plans or programs. And the qualifications for the label are infinitely elastic—you're someone who can make things change because you've been around for a while or because you're a fresh face, because you're an old Washington hand or because you're an outsider, because you're tough or because you're flexible. When I hear someone described as a change agent, I can't help recalling another meaning of *change*: as New Yorkers used to say, that and a nickel will get you on the subway.

CONVERSATION STOPPER

Fresh Air Commentary, April 2, 2008

=======

Just so we're straight on this: all that Barack Obama actually said in his speech in Philadelphia a few weeks ago was that "race is an issue that I believe this nation cannot afford to ignore right now." He didn't call for a national conversation or a national dialogue on race, or for that matter for a national discussion, debate, confabulation, or powwow.

Still, Obama didn't have to say the words for others to hear them. The *Los Angeles Times* praised him for "redefin[ing] our national conversation about race and politics," while the *Philadelphia Inquirer* asked, "Who better to lead a national conversation on the subject?" And Obama's conservative critics heard the same message, though they were more skeptical about the enterprise. In his *New York Times* column, William Kristol wrote, "The last thing we need now is a heated national conversation about race. . . . Let's not, and say we did."

But these days, it's natural to assume that any subject worth thinking about deserves to have a national conversation all its own. Hillary Clinton kicked off her campaign by announcing she was starting a national conversation about how to get the country back on track. Newt Gingrich has called for a national conversation on aging, and Condoleezza Rice has called for one on trade. And other people have issued appeals for national conversations about climate change, youth sports coaching, the future of classical music, marijuana laws, health care, and personalized learning.

Time was that when you said that Joe DiMaggio's hitting streak was a topic of national conversation, you merely meant that people were talking about it in bars and around water coolers from Maine to California. It was only about thirty years ago that people started to talk about a national conversation as a single coordinated chin-wag.

The phrase is meant to conjure up that famous Norman Rockwell painting of a New England town meeting, where ordinary citizens gather as equals to hash over the affairs of the day. Back in the 1930s, George Gallup claimed that polling and the modern media had re-created those meetings on a national scale—as he put it, "the nation is literally in one great room." Of course when you get that many people talking in one room, it's hard to tell if everybody is paying attention.

But by the time *national conversation* entered the language in the 1970s, the simulated public forum had become the model for a clutch of new media genres. In the 1976 presidential campaign, Jimmy Carter staged the first ersatz town meeting, the format that later found its Pavarotti in Bill Clinton. As it happens, that was also when Phil Donahue was pioneering tabloid talk TV, and Larry King launched the first national radio call-in show.

There was something reassuring about the idea of everybody participating in a vast extended conversation, particularly for a country trying to get past the angry divisions of Vietnam and the '60s. As the alternative therapies of the era were teaching us, no conflict was so rancorous that it couldn't be dispelled by open conversation, so long as people were honest about expressing their real feelings.

We probably shouldn't be calling these discussions "conversations" at all. A genuine conversation has no purpose—it's about the pleasures of merely circulating. The philosopher Michael Oakeshott said that an ideal conversation "has no determined course, we do not ask what it is 'for,' and we do not judge its excellence by its conclusion; it has no conclusion." It's always a little disconcerting when someone calls for a conversation about a specific topic. "We have to have a little conversation about all those late-night calls to Toledo." On the face of things, it sounds like a request for an open exchange of views, but you sense that most of the script has already been written.

But nowadays I keep hearing *conversation* used for exchanges that are entirely purposeful, particularly when they're designed to give people the impression that they're coming of their own free will to a conclusion that has actually been determined in advance. You get this a lot from consultants who earn a tough living by coming up with sentences like "We aim to lead the strategic conversation around value alignment." Not to be a stickler about it, but any discussion you can describe as strategic probably doesn't count as a conversation. The preposition itself gives the game away: *around* is the new *about*. "It's time for a new national conversation around health care." That isn't how we talk about our everyday chitchat: "We were just having a conversation around our favorite seafood joints."

And when you hear people call for a national conversation, you always know how they expect it to turn out. Every so often a foundation or the National Endowment for the Humanities will take the idea at face value and bring groups of citizens together in church basements or PBS stations for a heart-to-heart about race or American identity, but that rarely makes much of a ripple. And in any case, just calling for a national conversation usually makes the point all by itself. Both of the Clintons understand this, and so does Newt Gingrich. And William Bennett has called for half a dozen national conversations over the course of his career without ever feeling that he had to pretend to be a good listener.

Actually, what's usually most informative in all this is the debate about whether to have those conversations in the first place. If you really want to know what Americans think about race, type *national conversation* and *Obama* into Google News or one of the blog search engines. You'll get an earful, and the subject being race, the tone often falls short of what you'd call conversational. If we ever got to the point where we could really conduct a national conversation about race, we probably wouldn't need to.

THE REAL THING

Fresh Air Commentary, October 14, 2008

━━━━━━

I don't think there's ever been an era when politicians' speech and accents received so much critical scrutiny. During the primaries, a clip of Hillary Clinton's brief foray into Southern intonations made the rounds of the internet and cable shows under the heading "Kentucky Fried Hillary." Last January, William F. Buckley criticized John Edwards for manipulating audiences with a "carefully maintained Southern accent." Barack Obama has been knocked for occasionally falling into what some people called a "blackcent" that his upbringing didn't entitle him to. And even Michelle Obama was accused of pandering after her husband's surprise victory in the Iowa primary, when she said, "There ain't no blacks in Iowa."

It isn't just Democrats who come in for this. George W. Bush has been derided for exaggerating a West Texas twang that sounds nothing like the way his brother Jeb talks. And the reactions to Sarah Palin's speech mirror all the intense feelings she's aroused: it's grating, it's charming; it's illiterate, it's folksy; it's contrived, it's genuine.

You could pin some of that on the new media. Time was when candidates could tailor their speech to audiences in South Carolina or New York without having to worry that an audio clip of every *y'all* or *youse* would be instantly posted on the Web for the rest of the country to ponder.

But none of this would have any interest for us if accents didn't seem to offer a window on character. Mention someone's accent, and you unleash all the jargon of authenticity. Karl Rove charges that "[Hillary] calculates everything, including her accent and laugh." And Obama's linguistic shape-shifting led the African American conservative Shelby Steele to ask, "Who's the real [Obama]? What's his voice?"

If authenticity is a matter of heeding your true inner voice, then it probably isn't surprising that people listen for signs of it in the way you speak. So our notion of an authentic accent mirrors our idea of the authentic self. It's the natural speech you sucked up from the surroundings you grew up in, unfiltered and uncorrected. It's how you're supposed to sound when you're talking to yourself.

It's also a delusion. Or at least, if your speech is like yourself, it's because both are works in progress. My own speech covers a lot more territory than it did when I was growing up in a New York suburb. Sometimes it shifts toward what people would hear as East Coast nondescript. And sometimes it gets pretty sidewalks-of-New-York, particularly when I'm talking to friends from college days. (My sister once overheard me talking on the phone with one college friend and said, "Hey, what's with the 'awl' and 'cawl' business? You never used to talk that way.") But it doesn't make sense to ask what part of that is my "authentic" voice. You grow up; you meet new people; you change the way you talk. If you still sound the same way you did when you were fifteen, you haven't been getting out enough.

So what if George W. Bush came relatively late in life to west Texas and its g-dropping ways?* It's part of who he is now, and I'll bet it's how he sounds when somebody wakes him up in the middle of the night. And it's hard to imagine that Hillary could have spent fourteen years in a Little Rock law office without ever slipping into a drawl or that Obama could have worked on Chicago's South Side without picking up some of the local cadences. Shifting among accents isn't a sign of a fragmented self, but only of a well-traveled one. (Though in the age of YouTube, it's probably ill-advised to do it during a national campaign.)

Of course there are politicians who don't feel the need to tailor their accents to their audience, like John McCain and Joe Biden. Maybe that's a sign of their inner constancy, or maybe it's just because they aren't really trying to create the illusion of a personal relationship with the audience that the others are after.

But linguistic authenticity is a different matter for politicians who have rural or popular roots, like Bill Clinton and Sarah Palin. Lionel Trilling described *authentic* as a kind of moral slang, and the word is usually laced with condescension. It implies quaintness or local color; it's a word we use for creole cooking or dim sum, not haute cuisine. And when people talk about authentic accents, they're not thinking of the way people speak on the TV news or in middle-class suburbs, but of the

---

*Linguists dislike the term *g-dropping*. The fact is that phonetically there is no *g* in these words—we don't say "huntinG or fishinG"—and the process actually involves the substitution of one nasal consonant for another.

speech in places like South Philly and Fargo, not to mention Hot Springs, Arkansas, and Wasilla, Alaska. Nobody would ask whether Brian Williams's accent is authentic—actually a lot of people would say he doesn't have an accent at all. (When I hear someone described as having no accent, I think of those pinkish Crayola crayons we used to have that were labeled "flesh.")

So like Bill Clinton, Palin can signal authenticity simply by refashioning her original accent, rather than acquiring a new one. You can actually hear how this developed if you pull up the YouTube video of Palin as a twenty-four-year-old Anchorage sportscaster fresh from her broadcasting classes in college. She wasn't in control of her accent back then: she scattered the desk with dropped *g*'s: "Purdue was killin' Michigan." "Look what they're doin' to Chicago." It's strikingly different from the way she talks now in her public appearances, not just because she's much more poised, but because she's learned how to work it. When she talks about policy, her *g*'s are decorously in place — she never says "reducin' taxes" or "cuttin' spendin'." But the *g*'s disappear when she speaks on behalf of ordinary Americans— "Americans are cravin' something different," or "People . . . are hurtin' 'cause the economy is hurtin'." It's of a piece with the *you betchas*, *doggones*, and other effusions that are calculated to signal spontaneous candor.

Now there are clearly a lot of people who find this engaging, but I can't imagine that anybody really supposes it's artless. What it is, rather, is a stone-washed impersonation of a Matanuska-Susitna Valley girl. I wouldn't be surprised if Palin and her friends perfected this way back in high school. There's no group that's so unself-conscious that its members don't get a kick out of parodying their own speech: most Brooklynites do a very creditable Brooklyn, and every student at St. Paul's and Choate can do a dead-on preppie lockjaw. And with all credit to Tina Fey, she wouldn't be so brilliant at doing Sarah Palin if Sarah Palin weren't so good at doing herself.

THE ISM DISMALEST OF ALL

Fresh Air Commentary, October 29, 2008

═══════

The most striking thing about the McCain campaign's claim that Obama is a socialist is that they had to thrash through so many other charges before they got around to it. Obama is inexperienced; he's all talk; he's a defeatist; he's an out-of-touch elitist; he's a celebrity. He'll say anything to get elected; he hangs out with a former terrorist. Then, finally: Oh yeah, and did we mention he's a socialist?

Time was when that was always the first charge Republicans turned to when someone proposed increasing the role or power of government. The income tax, child labor laws, Social Security, FDIC, the Civil Rights Act of 1948—to Republicans they were all either "socialistic" or "creeping socialism," a phrase coined by Thomas Dewey in 1939. Democrats found this maddening—in 1952, Harry Truman called *socialism* a scare word and said that when a Republican said, "Down with socialism!" he really meant "Down with progress!"

But it was only with the eclipse of liberalism and the decline and breakup of international communism that the charges of socialism began to yield to a new anti–big-government rhetoric in Republicans' public pronouncements. Ronald Reagan taught the Republicans that the Washington bureaucrat can be made to look scary enough without having to paint him as an incipient commissar. These days, *creeping socialism* has been consigned to the dustbin of history, and *socialistic* is heard mostly on talk radio and in conservative blogs. True, Republicans routinely raise the danger of socialized medicine. But as best I can tell, neither George W. Bush nor Dick Cheney has ever used the words *socialist* or *socialism* in the context of American politics while they were in office. And while Rudy Giuliani has charged in interviews that Hillary Clinton supports socialism, neither he nor any other speaker used the word in addressing the Republican National Convention, nor does it appear on the Web site of the Republican National Committee.

So why was the McCain campaign tempted to resuscitate the charge? It may be that *liberal* has been so saturated with effete cultural stereotypes that it didn't have enough impact when the conversation turned to economics. Or maybe the idea is that *socialist* itself has become so unusual in electoral politics that it has started to sound sinister and exotic. You could have that impression when you hear the calls of "He's a socialist!" when Obama is mentioned at McCain and Palin rallies. It's hard to imagine people at Democratic rallies yelling "He's a supply-sider!" when McCain's name comes up.

The politically engaged on both sides have tended to evaluate the charge literally. Conservatives parse Obama's statements to discern any traces of Marxist ideology; liberals ridicule the idea that increasing the marginal tax rate by 3 percent somehow crosses the line to collectivism.

But this isn't about definitions. An old-time Republican conservative like Robert A. Taft might have been surprised to hear the party's vice presidential candidate say, "Now is not the time to experiment with socialism" at the same time the ticket was endorsing the partial nationalization of the banks and urging Congress to buy up troubled mortgages. But it has been more than seventy years since anybody thought that socialism might be a serious political alternative in America, and since then the power of the word has been symbolic, not substantive. As Walter Lippmann once put it, it's one of those words that are meant to "assemble emotions after they have been detached from their ideas." To most Americans, the emotions that *socialism* stirs up have always had less to do not just with political theories but with the eclectic cast of characters the word has brought to mind from one era to the next: bomb-throwing radicals, supercilious parlor pinks, insidious subversives, Soviet thugs, third-world guerillas, pretentious French intellectuals.

To Joe the Plumber and a lot of other people, the thought of socialism is still chilling—the ism dismalest of all, as the Chad Mitchell Trio put it in a 1962 song. The question is whether evoking that prospect will help McCain to make his case against Obama's tax plan among independent and undecided voters. Does the specter of socialism still haunt those who aren't party to the conversations of the right?

Probably not. Earlier this year the Harvard School of Public Health reported the results of a survey of American attitudes about socialized medicine. It turned out that more people said that socialized medicine would improve the health care system than said it would make things worse. And among people under thirty-five, the proportion of those who approved of socialized medicine was almost two to one. Not that most of those people have a clear understanding of socialized medicine, or of socialism itself, for that matter. Americans have always been a little fuzzy on that concept (these days, it seems as if Europeans are, too). But if you were seven years old when the Berlin Wall fell, the word *socialism* probably isn't going to sound very toxic—you're more likely to think of Tony Blair's England than the Soviet gulags.

Alexis de Tocqueville said that the last thing a party abandons is its language. But it doesn't happen all at once. Before a language dies, it becomes what linguists call a hearth language: it's no longer used in the wider world but still spoken by old women around the kitchen table. Or in this case, on the blogs and radio shows that serve as kitchen tables in the world of modern politics.

The left has a hearth language of its own, the discarded limbs of the heyday of liberalism. Fifty or sixty years ago, no Democrat could finish a speech without denouncing the Republicans as reactionaries. Now the word is barely a tenth as frequent in the press as it was then, and it doesn't appear at all in the pages that the Democratic National Committee posts at its Web site. But it still gets thousands of hits at sites like the Huffington Post and Daily Kos, where liberals keep it on life support.

The hearth language of the right is where you find the vocabulary of old-guard anticommunism preserved in aspic— *Bolshevik, cradle-to-grave, socialistic.* Or take *class warfare.* It's still the first term that conservatives reach for whenever Democrats suggest that the wealthy aren't paying their share. But it has been a long time since it could conjure up images of workers in cloth caps throwing up barricades in the street.

Surveying the debris of the Soviet empire in 1991, Irving Kristol, the godfather of neoconservatism, announced, "Communism is over. And that means that anticommunism is over, too." Linguistically, it has taken a while for that to sink in.

JUST A THING CALLED JOE

Fresh Air Commentary, December 22, 2008

━━━━━━━

Ever since the "word of the year" business was started by the American Dialect Society in 1990, people have had different ideas about what the qualifications for the honor should be. Some look for a clever or timely neologism. This year the editors of the *Oxford American Dictionary* chose *hypermiling,* which refers to trying to get maximum mileage out of your car. It hasn't exactly become a household word, but it'll be handy to have around the next time gas goes over four bucks a gallon. William Safire picked *frugalista,* another item that captures the pinchpenny Zeitgeist, even if it sounds as if it were rescued from the wastebasket in the *Colbert Report* writers' room. And *Webster's New World Dictionary* chose *oversharing* for divulging excessive personal information. That one has actually been around since the early '90s, but then, lexicographers are a little slow on the uptake.

I prefer to go with those who look for a word that encapsulates some major story of the year, particularly in a year as epochal as this one. The editors of *Merriam-Webster's* chose *bailout,* the word that got the biggest spike in lookups on the dictionary's Web site (my guess is that it's also the word that figured most prominently in the captions of *New Yorker* cartoons, which is probably a more telling indicator). And you could certainly make an argument for *change* or *post-racial* or *collateral debt obligation,* to name a few. But none of those is particularly interesting as a word. If it were up to me, I'd fasten on the brief resurgence of *Joe,* a name that encapsulates the whole history of twentieth-century populism.

In 1942, FDR's vice president Henry Wallace made a famous speech in which he declared we were living in "the century of the common man." For most of that century the common man went by the name of Joe. The generic Joe Blow first showed up in the 1920s, along with his aliases Joe Bloggs and Joe Zilch, to be joined later by Joe Schmo from Kokomo. And by the '30s *Joe* had replaced *John* and *Jack* as a generic word for a chap or a fellow, as in *a good Joe* or *a regular Joe.* Perhaps that was because *Joe* seemed more ethnically inclusive and urban than *John*— Josephs have always been thicker on the ground in New York than in Arkansas.*

GI Joe made his first appearance in 1942 as a comic-strip character in the Army weekly *Yank.* He quickly took the place of Johnny Doughboy, a holdover from World War I. Since that period *Joe* has always been the name people reached for when they wanted to suggest blue-collar unpretentiousness. You

---

*That may explain why *John* continued to be used generically in the itinerant's derisive *John Farmer.* *John* is also used in *John Q. Public,* which is more classless than the roughly equivalent *Joe Citizen.* Most languages seem to have a proper name that can be used generically—in Italian it's Tizio, in Spanish it's Fulano or Juan Perez, in Latin it was Gaius, and in Dutch it's Jan, as in Jan Boezeroen (John Overalls), meaning "workman," and Jantje Beton (Johnny Cement), "inner-city child."

think of Joe Palooka, the affable heavyweight champ from a popular comic strip that dated from the '30s, or Jackie Gleason's garrulous Joe the bartender, or Josephine the plumber, who was featured in long-running ads for Comet cleanser in the 1960s. Joe Camel slouched onto the scene a couple of decades later, shooting pool with his baseball cap on backwards or sitting on his motorcycle in a black leather jacket, always with a cigarette dangling from his split lip. Man or dromedary, you couldn't imagine him as a Jeremy.

Joes don't stand on ceremony, which is why the truncation is compulsory for any politician called Joseph, particularly if he can claim modest origins. Hey, can I call you Joe? Actually, that's sort of the idea.

Joe Lunchpail appeared in the 1960s, and Safire has traced Joe Sixpack back to a 1970 Boston congressional race. At the time, some people heard the phrase as a slur on Irish voters, but it caught on as a slightly jocular handle for ordinary working-class Americans—Homer Simpson embraced the label and expanded on it, calling himself "a regular Joe Twelve-Pack."

Those are the voters both parties have been wooing since the late 1960s, but usually under oblique labels like *the silent majority*, *working Americans*, or *the forgotten middle class*. (The working class and lower middle class have no entries in the American political lexicon.) Pundits and politicos on both sides might endlessly chew over the question "What does Joe Sixpack want?" but the gentleman was referred to only in the third person. Before Sarah Palin, no national candidates had ever addressed Joe Sixpack by name, much less offered themselves as a representative of what Palin called "the normal Joe Sixpack American."

And then in one of those you-can't-make-this-stuff-up moments, the NJSA constituency acquired a flesh-and-blood embodiment in the form of an Ohio man who happened to go by his middle name of Joe and who worked in the canonical twentieth-century blue-collar job. (He was also a dead ringer for Peter Boyle in his title role as a hippie-hating factory worker in the 1970 movie *Joe*). That was pure serendipity—there's no way Wurzelbacher would have been transformed into a campaign mascot if he'd been Dwayne the drywall guy.

Between the mediagenic double-teaming of Joe the Plumber and the Joe Sixpack–identified vice presidential candidate, Republicans' populist pitch was more explicit and energetic than at any time since Nixon and Agnew ignited the culture wars forty years ago. Their partisans were adrenalized, piling into Palin's rallies with placards bearing their first names and job descriptions. But outside of the Republican base, there was no rush to enroll in the Joe Sixpack nation. Of course there are lots of reasons for that. Some had feared that Palin might incarnate Joe Sixpack a little too authentically, and Joe the Plumber turned out to be something of a loose spigot. And then most people simply had a number of other things on their minds this year. But whatever candidates happen to be carrying the Republican standard in 2012, it isn't likely they'll be bringing along any of this year's Joes when they make their way back to Ohio and Pennsylvania.

That's the risk of populist rhetoric: what sounds plain-folks in one ear will sound patronizing in another. Notwithstanding Henry Wallace's glorious speech or Aaron Copland's even more glorious fanfare, the common man has never been crazy about being referred to as the common man. And with the notable exception of Homer Simpson, most people aren't comfortable having their sociopolitical identity reduced to a beverage preference, whether it's for beer or chardonnay. Americans may still feel a nostalgic affection for the picturesque working-class characters the name Joe evoked in the last century. But when they catch a glimpse of themselves in a mirror—well, it's funny, but they don't look Joeish.

ENGLISH 2.0

BLOGGING IN THE GLOBAL LUNCHROOM

Fresh Air Commentary, April 20, 2004

———

Over the last couple of months, I've been posting on a group blog called Language Log, which was launched by a couple of linguists as a place where we could vent our comments on the passing linguistic scene.

I don't yet have the hang of the form. The style that sounds perfectly normal in a public radio feature or an op-ed piece comes off as distant and pontifical when I use it in a blog entry. Reading over my own postings, I recall what Queen Victoria once said about Gladstone: "He speaks to me as if I were a public meeting."

I'm not the only one with this problem. A lot of newspapers have been encouraging or even requiring their writers to start blogs. But with some notable exceptions, most journalists have the same problems that I do. They do all the things you should do in a newspaper feature. They fashion engaging ledes, they develop their arguments methodically, they give context and background, and they tack helpful IDs onto the names they introduce—"New York Senator Charles E. Schumer (D)."

That makes for solid journalism, but it's not really blogging. Granted, that word can cover a lot of territory. A recent Pew Foundation study found that around 3 million Americans have tried their hands at blogging, and sometimes there seem to be almost that many variants of the form. Blogs can be news summaries, opinion columns, or collections of press releases, like the official blogs of the presidential candidates. But the vast majority are journals posted by college students, office workers, or stay-at-home moms, whose average readership is smaller than a family Christmas letter.

But when people puzzle over the significance of blogs nowadays, they usually have in mind a small number of A-List sites that traffic in commentary about politics, culture, gossip, or technology—blogs like Altercation, Instapundit, Matthew Yglesias, Andrew Sullivan, Talking Points Memo, or Doc Searls. It's true that bloggers like these have occasionally come up with news scoops, but in the end they're less about breaking stories than bending them. And their language is a kind of anti-journalese. It's informal, impertinent, and digressive, casting links in all directions. In fact one archetypal blog entry consists entirely of a cryptic comment that's linked to another blog or a news item—"Talk about pale imitations," or "Why are the Dems talking about this instead of about this?"

That interconnectedness is what leads enthusiasts to talk about the blogosphere, as if this were all a single vast conversation—at some point in these discussions, somebody's likely to trot out the phrase *collective mind*. But if there's a new public sphere assembling itself out there, you couldn't tell from the way bloggers address their readers—not as anonymous citizens, the way print columnists do, but as coconspirators who are in on the joke.

Taken as a whole, in fact, the blogging world sounds a lot less like a public meeting than the lunchtime chatter in a high-school cafeteria, complete with snarky comments about the kids at the tables across the room. (Bloggers didn't invent the word *snarky*, but they've had a lot to do with turning it into the metrosexual equivalent of *bitchy*.)

Some people say this all started with Mickey Kaus's column in *Slate*, though Kaus himself cites the old *San Francisco Chronicle* columns of Herb Caen. And Camille Paglia not surprisingly claims that her column on Salon.com was the first true blog and adds that the genre has been going downhill ever since. But blogs were around on the Web well before Kaus or Paglia first logged in. And if you're of a mind to, you can trace their print antecedents a lot further back than Caen or Hunter S. Thompson. That informal style recalls the colloquial voice that Addison and Steele devised when they invented the periodical essay in the early eighteenth century, even if few blogs come close to them in artfulness. Then too, those essays were written in the guise of fictive personae like Isaac Bickerstaff and Sir Roger de Coverly, who could be the predecessors of pseudonymous bloggers like Wonkette, Atrios, or Skippy the Bush Kangaroo.

For that matter, my Language Log co-contributor Mark Liberman recalls that Plato always had Socrates open his philosophical disquisitions with a little diary entry, the way bloggers like to do: "I went down yesterday to see the festival at the Peiraeus with Glaucon, the son of Ariston, and I ran into my old buddy Cephalus, and we got to talking about old age. . . . "

Of course whenever a successful new genre emerges, it seems to have been implicit in everything that preceded it. But in the end, this is a mug's game, like asking whether the first SUV was a minivan, a station wagon, or an off-road vehicle.

The fact is that this is a genuinely new language of public discourse—and a paradoxical one. On the one hand, blogs are clearly a more democratic form of expression than anything the world of print has produced. But in some ways they're also more exclusionary, and not just because they only reach about a tenth of the people who use the Web. The high, formal style of the newspaper op-ed page may be nobody's native language, but at least it's a neutral voice that doesn't privilege the speech of any particular group or class. Whereas blogspeak is basically an adaptation of the table talk of the urban middle class—it isn't a language that everybody in the cafeteria is equally adept at speaking. Not that there's anything wrong with chewing over the events of the day with the other folks at the lunch table, but you hope that everybody in the room is at least starting the day with the same newspapers.

TOUCHED BY THE TURN OF A PAGE

Los Angeles Times, December 19, 2004

———

The announcement last week that Google would begin digitizing the collections of several major research libraries evoked a memory from my graduate student days at the University of Pennsylvania. I was trying to find a journal in the library stacks when I happened on a 1929 book by Sterling Leonard on eighteenth-century doctrines of English usage. The card in the pocket inside the back cover showed that it had last been checked out twelve years earlier by the great medievalist Albert C. Baugh, reason enough to give it a look.

Some years later, I sought out Leonard's book in the Stanford University library and found that that copy also held a yellowing card with Baugh's delicate signature. It left me wondering whether every library in the world was holding a copy of Leonard's book on its shelves just in case Albert C. Baugh or I happened to find ourselves in the neighborhood some time.

That's the vision of the ubiquitous universal library that scholars and technologists have been dreaming of since 1945, when Vannevar Bush conceived the Memex machine, a theoretical analog computer that could display all the books in the library at a scholar's desk. With the development of the World Wide Web, that prospect came to seem plausible. In 1995, IBM ran a commercial that showed an Italian farmer proudly explaining to his granddaughter that he had just gotten his degree remotely from Indiana University, which had put its entire library online with help from IBM. A lot of people took the conversion as a done deal, and the university librarian was obliged to explain that, to date, only a fraction of the library's music collection had been digitized.

A great many scholarly and scientific journals have come online since then. But to most people, a library still means books: the Google announcement signals that the virtual library has become a reality, even if it will be a while in the making. It will take a decade to digitize 15 million books and documents from the Stanford and University of Michigan libraries, and more time than that before most other research collections are online. And although readers will have full access to books in the public domain, they won't be able to view more than a few pages of books that are still under copyright.

In the scenario of that IBM ad, the digitization of library collections seemed destined to obviate the need for paper books and brick-and-mortar libraries. As Al Gore described the vision in 1984, "I want a schoolchild in Carthage, Tenn., to come to school and be able to plug into the Library of Congress."

By now, though, people have begun to realize that what that Carthage schoolchild needs most is still a neighborhood public library, even if it's a small one. When you're ten years old, it doesn't take a huge collection to convince you that the world holds more books than you could ever read.

And the research library also has a continuing role to play. Scholars and scientists may be dazzled by the prospect of universal access to the world's research collections, but the librarians who made the accord with Google don't feel as if they're presiding over the dissolution of their bookish empires.

This semester, I co-taught a graduate course at the Berkeley School of Information Systems and Management. The fifteen or so people in the class were probably the most wired students at a very wired university in this wired corner of the world. But when I asked on the last day of class how many of them had visited the university library the previous week, two-thirds raised their hands, and all of them said they'd been there over the course of the semester.

That isn't surprising. For one thing, physical libraries facilitate the sort of serendipitous encounter I had with Leonard's monograph, even if barcodes and privacy concerns have sadly eliminated those cards with the names of previous borrowers. Most scholars will tell you that a lot of the most interesting books they've read are ones they happened on when they were looking for something else. Searchable digitized texts are ideal for finding a reference or locating a particular passage. And they can make for their own kind of serendipitous browsing, provided you're willing to sort through a lot of chaff—pull down all the nineteenth-century books and periodicals that talk about "manners" and "vulgarity," say, and you'll learn quite a bit about Victorian social attitudes.

But it's hard to get an overall sense of a book when you're barreling into it sideways. And for sustained reading, digital texts can't provide the sense of place we have when we read a paper book, unconsciously measuring our progress by the diminishing distance between our thumb and forefinger—the "tell-tale compression of the pages," as Jane Austen put it in *Northanger Abbey*, that signals that "we are all hastening together to perfect felicity." You become aware of that sense of place when you're looking for a particular passage in a biography or novel you read recently and recall that it was about halfway in, on the bottom half of a left-hand page—not a spatial perception you're likely to have when you read an extended text on a laptop or a handheld. Reading Proust in a browser window, I once observed, is like touring Normandy through a bombsight—though that absence of context matters a lot less if you're reading a book of recipes or Raymond Carver stories.

That's one reason why it's likely that book publishers will relax restrictions on viewing digital versions of copyrighted books. The evidence suggests that providing free access to large portions of books can often help their print sales. There are only two reasons for buying a book, after all. Either we intend to read it, in which case most of us find a printed version preferable, or we don't intend to read it, in which case a printed version is absolutely essential.

Still, there are risks to putting research collections online. The cost of digitizing large research collections is too great to permit a second pass, and the job has to be done to technical standards that will be adequate not just for today's purposes, but for technologies fifty years in the future. (The French learned that lesson in 1993, when they inaugurated their new national library by digitizing a large collection of books at what turned out to be a poor image quality.) And no one is quite sure yet that we'll be able to preserve digital records for anything like the lifetime of a paper book.

Then too, the advent of the virtual research library will no doubt increase the already strong pressures to cut back on library services, "de-acquisition" portions of expensive-to-maintain collections, or even eliminate some libraries entirely—"You've got all that stuff online now."

That would be a pity. The virtual library realizes the fantasy of universal access that I had many years ago: Sterling Leonard's seminal monograph will be available to me not just from Penn and Stanford, but if I happen to find myself in Carthage, Tennessee. But if that's all there is, think of all the books we'll never stumble on as we potter around in the shelves.

Postscript, January 2009: Late in 2008, four years after Google announced the project then called Google Print, the company reached an agreement with the Association of American Publishers and the Authors Guild that would permit the digitization of copyrighted works. Although that removed one obstacle to the vision of the universal library, most of those works will be available to the public only in an effectively useless "snippet view." Yet even if you consider only the several million public domain works that are available on full view or the copyrighted works that are available—sometimes quite extensively—in "limited view," the project has already exceeded some expectations. For students and researchers, it's a lot easier to find discussions of a specific topic than it would be if you were constrained to leaf through the indexes of the works in a physical collection one by one. When my daughter was writing a paper on Jimi Hendrix's Woodstock performance of "The Star-Spangled Banner" for her American Studies course at Wellesley, she used Google Books to find relevant critical discussions, rather than having to rely on press stories and amateurish Web sites, and on occasion went to get the book in its entirety from the college library so as to be able to read it properly. (Rereading this piece now, it strikes me that I didn't make it clear enough that there's more than one way to stumble over a book.) There are other obvious advantages. Google Books makes it easier to evaluate prospective purchases: at a rough estimate, I've bought at least fifty books in the last couple of years after I previewed them on Google Books. And not that it means much to anybody else, but we linguists are delighted to have a huge corpus of historical works to search over when we're trying to track down, say, the origin of *Johnny Doughboy*.

On the other hand, Google Books already has some very serious limitations, although a few require only technological improvements. The viewing software makes reading texts a lot more difficult than it has to be (by comparison, take a look at the stunning viewer that the nonprofit Internet Archive makes available for the million or so digitized books in its digital collection). More seriously, the quality of scanning, indexing, and cataloguing is too often poor. Pages are often missing, blurred, or blocked by the image of the scanner operator's fingers. The data about the works are almost never as useful as what you would get from a good library catalogue; books are listed under completely erroneous titles and authors; works are misdated by twenty or fifty years.

People have tried to defend the project by pointing out that that's how new systems always evolve: "We'll get it out there now and fix it later." But fixing these errors will take a long time—actually, it will take a very long time just to spot and report them all—and it will cost more to repair them than it would have cost to get it right from the outset.

To fill in the missing pages in the introduction of the 1809 edition of James Templeman's long narrative poem *Gilbert*, for example, somebody at the Oxford University Libraries is going to have to find the book on a shelf and pull it down again, scan the missing pages, reinsert the page images in the electronic file, and put the book back on the shelves, all of which will cost about as much as it cost to scan the book in the first place. And the same procedure will have to be followed to correct the badly scanned pages and other errors that Paul Duguid, my colleague at the Berkeley School of Information, found in the full-text editions of *Tristram Shandy* scanned for Google Books by the Harvard and Stanford libraries.

Many of these problems could probably have been avoided if there had been a more concerted effort to plan and coordinate the building of the digital library from the outset, as there has been in some European nations. On the other hand, centralized planning has its own pitfalls, as the French never tire of demonstrating. And Google deserves the credit for undertaking the project with no clear idea of how they were going to make money from it. (My guess is that they'll come up with something.)

LOWERCASING THE INTERNET

San Jose Mercury News, October 17, 2008

Most people didn't take much notice when the editors of Wired News announced recently that they had decided to drop the capital letter on *Internet* and *Web*. But the news had the tech world burning the midnight phosphor. Techie bloggers reacted indignantly, and there were more than eight hundred comments posted on Slashdot, the Web site that serves geeks as a digital water cooler. To listen to a lot of them, it was as if the *New Yorker* had announced that the figure of Eustace Tilley on its anniversary issue cover would be replacing his top hat with a do-rag.

Still, in the natural course of things, it was probably inevitable that *Internet* and *Web* would ultimately lose their capital letters. Back in the 1920s, people sometimes capitalized *the Radio* and *the Cinema*, but they stopped doing that when the media receded into the cultural background. That was what led Wired to go to the lowercase forms—as the editors put it, it was a way of acknowledging that the Internet is simply "another medium for delivering and receiving information."

Not that the minusculization of *Web* and *Internet* will happen overnight. The uppercase forms are pretty much universal in the press, and those are the versions that are recommended in most stylebooks and dictionaries (including the 2000 edition of the *American Heritage*, for whom I wrote a usage note that recommended the capitalized form).

Of course you could say that asking a decidedly old-media authority like a dictionary or the *Associated Press Stylebook* to rule on the spelling of *Internet* is like asking the *Harvard Dictionary of Music* to rule on the correct spelling of hip-hop slang. But it isn't just the usage authorities that lead people to capitalize *Internet* and *Web*. As all those postings to Slashdot testify, there's a strong sense that these words merit the distinction. That may be why a lot of newspapers and Web sites capitalize *blogosphere*, too, even though it isn't mentioned in any dictionary or style guide yet.

Why the insistence on capitalizing *Internet*? Old hands like to point out that the word was once used as a common noun for a collection of networks that shared a common communications protocol—what we call *the Internet* started out as only one of many. But by itself, that wouldn't turn the name into a proper noun. After all, we don't capitalize *the Power Grid*, which was also just one of many once.

The real reason people insist on capitalizing the words is that they like to think of them on the model of other common nouns that have been elevated to the proper names of specific places, names like the Shire, the Channel, and the Coast. Bill Thompson, a commentator on technology for the BBC, writes that "those who choose 'internet' over 'Internet' are as wrong as those who would visit london, meet the queen or go for a boat trip down the river thames."

That picture of the Internet owes something to our propensity for conceiving of the medium in a spatial way. Back in the salad days of cyberspace, the digital world was usually depicted as an open expanse like an ocean, a plain, or a galaxy—or sometimes, all of the above. As one visionary put it in 1991, cyberspace is "a territory swarming with data and lies, with mind stuff and memories of nature. The realm of pure information, filling like a lake."

After a while, of course, that conception of the Internet as a virtual Great Plains began to yield to one of a virtual Bowery, as settlers started to stake out the territory and its geography acquired features more typical of an urban landscape, like portals, gateways, and sites. But the language we use to talk about the Internet is always uniquely spatial. We don't talk about visiting a novel or going to the TV news.

Still, you can think of the Internet as a space without thinking of it as a particular place. We could regard it as one of those ubiquitous presences like the atmosphere or the cosmos, names we feel no urge to dignify with capital letters. The capital letter turns the Internet into a specific locale—not a physical place, of course, but a social one. It implies a conurbation where a single extended community is taking form—sort of a virtual Santa Clara, only with cheaper rentals.

That notion of a single community is implicit in the phrases that cyber-visionaries like to toss around when they're talking about the online world—*emerging consciousness, social contract, netizens,* and *collective mind.* Or as John Perry Barlow put it in a manifesto that betrays a stylistic debt to Robert Heinlein: "I come from Cyberspace, the new home of Mind. On behalf of the future, I ask you of the past to leave us alone. . . . You do not know us, nor did you create the wealth of our market-places. You have not engaged in our great and gathering con-versation. . . . We will create a civilization of the Mind in Cyberspace."

Listening to that, your first thought is apt to be, "What do you mean, 'we'?" When it comes to the crunch, the Internet is no more a coherent community than the collection of travelers who happen to find themselves in O'Hare airport on a given Monday afternoon on their way to Stuttgart, San Juan, or St. Louis.

If the Internet permits the illusion of community, it's only because we don't have to actually rub elbows with most other travelers there. We move around in it the way Donald Trump cruises around New York, alighting from the limo only when we pull up at a destination full of people just like us.

But if you want a demonstration of just how jumbled the voices in cyberspace are, visit one of the sites called "voyeurs," which throw up a random selection of queries as they come in to the search engines. *Cape May hotels, Anna Kournikova, pro death penalty, mapa de Galápagos, Aston Kutcher filmography, Bush de-ception, loans until payday, scavenger fish jokes, Israel atrocities. . . .*

Taken together, it makes for a sort of *poésie concrète*. But if that's the product of a collective mind, it's a mighty scattered one. All the more reason for writing *internet* with a lowercase *i*. It reminds you that there really is no out there out there.

TEACHING STUDENTS TO SWIM IN THE ONLINE SEA

New York Times, February 13, 2005

―――――――

Information literacy is a catchphrase whose time has come. Last month, the Educational Testing Service announced that it had developed a test to measure students' ability to do online research—as close as you could get to official acknowledgment that the millions spent to wire schools and universities is of little use unless students know how to retrieve the information they need from the oceans of sludge on the Web.

A quarter century after the personal computer made its appearance, it's clear that "computer skills" are not enough, no more than gold prospecting can be reduced to dexterity with a pick and hammer—the real challenge is to assay the lumps that a search dislodges. A friend of mine who teaches Scandinavian literature at Berkeley recently described the way her students use the Web to research a paper on the Vikings: "They're Berkeley students, so of course, they have the sense to restrict their searches to 'vikings NOT Minnesota.' But they're perfectly willing to believe a Web site about early Viking settlements in Oklahoma."

That credulity is largely a legacy of the print age. If we're disposed to trust what we read in library books, it is because they've been screened twice: first by a publisher who decided they were worth printing, and then by the librarian who acquired them or the professor who requested their purchase. But the Web eliminates those filters, even as it allows us to research subjects we would never have gone to a traditional library for, from planning a vacation to shopping for a date or a digital camera. For a lot of adolescents, in fact, the internet is most valuable as a source of information about concerns that they're reluctant to discuss with parents or teachers, like sexual behavior, sexual identity, drug use, or depression and suicide.

But there's a paradox in the way people think of the Web. Everyone is aware that it's teeming with mistakes and misinformation, puffery and poppycock, sleaze and slander—what you could lump as "rotten information." Yet most people feel confident that they can sort out the dross. In a survey released last month by the Pew Project on the Internet and American Life, 87 percent of search-engine users said they found what they were looking for all or most of the time.

That's partly because a lot of the information we search for is easy to find and self-evident, like a movie schedule or the current temperature in Miami. But when a search involves evaluating more complex or subjective material, that high level of confidence isn't particularly reassuring. According to the Pew survey, only 38 percent of search-engine users were aware of the difference between unpaid and sponsored search results, and only 18 percent could tell which was which.

A 2002 study directed by BJ Fogg, a Stanford psychologist, found that people tend to judge the credibility of a Web site by its appearance, rather than by checking who put it up and why. But it is much easier to produce a professional-looking Web site than a credible-looking book or magazine. The BBC was recently duped by a fake Dow Chemical site into broadcasting an interview with an environmentalist posing as a company spokesman.

Then, too, search engines make it all too easy to filter information in ways that reinforce preexisting biases. A Google search on *homosexual marriage*, for example, will turn up popular Web pages that feature those words prominently, most of which will oppose same-sex marriage and will link to other sites that have the same point of view. Substitute the query *gay marriage*, and you'll come up with a very different set of pages. A researcher exploring the same topic in a library would be more likely to encounter diverse points of view.

Up to now, librarians have taken the lead in developing information literacy standards and curricula. There's a certain irony in that, since a lot of people assumed that the "disintermediation" of information would leave both libraries and librarians with no role to play. (*"Librarians?* Where we're going we don't *need* librarians.")

But these days the school librarian—if the school still has one—is often just a relief teacher overwhelmed with administrative chores. And college students tend to have contact with librarians only during the obligatory freshman library tour, in which they're instructed in the intricacies of the Dewey Decimal system, or when they visit the library's understaffed help desk. For the most part, they do their online information seeking at home or in the dorm, with no one to guide them.

Then too, consigning the problem to librarians alone rein-
forces a misapprehension that's implicit in the term *information literacy* itself. *Literacy* is a deceptively capacious word. No
other language has a single term that spans the basic ability to
read and write, a general familiarity with culture, and a mini-
mal competence in a particular subject. When we talk about *ge-
ographical literacy* or *economic literacy*, it's with the implication
that a subject can be condensed to a list of elementary ABCs
and relegated to a module with a specific course number.

That picture can be reductive even for subject matters like
geography or economics, but it's particularly risky to speak of
literacy in a broad notion like culture or information. *Information literacy* presumes that students can be implanted with a
kind of virtual pineal gland that will serve them equally well
in any context—researching a paper on Alexander Hamilton,
shopping for a laptop, or finding online suicide counseling.

To a lot of people, *information literacy* suggests a set of basic
principles consigned to a new course called Information 101
or tacked on as an extra unit at the end of a freshman composition course. And in fact people tend to expand the term into
lists of general principles like "Evaluate sources critically";
"Check to see if the site sponsor is reputable"; and "Look for
evidence of bias." But vague precepts like those are of no more
use than a consumer advice site that urges car buyers to "select
a reliable model" and "try to get the best price from the dealer."
Shopping isn't a skill you can teach in the abstract.

Last fall, for example, I co-taught a graduate course on "Information Quality" at Berkeley's School of Information Management and Systems. However you define information literacy,

our students had it in spades. They were at ease with the technology and knowledgeable about how search engines work and how their results can be misleading. But even those students had difficulty when we asked them to evaluate information in unfamiliar areas, like using the Web to decide which online degree program to recommend to a friend with certain needs.

In fact navigating the internet is no different from navigating the world on the other side of the screen—your adroitness in cruising the interstate won't necessarily help you find your way back to your hotel in Rome. Whether in the print or the online world, information literacy invariably includes a large helping of subject-specific strategies and knowledge. Sometimes it's a question of knowing where to go for information in a particular area. University librarians are always complaining that students confine their research to Google, ignoring the useful and often expensive digital resources that the libraries have acquired, from collections of eighteenth-century newspapers to census data to bibliographic databases on waterfowl.

Or very often, the trick is knowing whom to ask about a topic. Email turns the Web into a vast digital help desk; user groups and discussion lists are full of people who will gladly explain the metallurgy of espresso machine boilers or the history of English slang. Back in 1989, I emailed a colleague to ask if he could locate a certain source for me. He replied that he'd been able to find the reference on a new network called the World Wide Web and added, "I once had a professor who said that knowing something was the same thing as knowing where to look for it, so I guess I knew it all along." "In that case," I answered, "I guess I did too."

In the end, instruction in information literacy will have to pervade every level of education and every course in the curriculum, from historians' use of collections of online slave narratives to middle-school home economics teachers showing their students where to find reliable nutrition information on the Web. Even then, it is true, most people will fall back on perfunctory techniques for finding and evaluating information online. As BJ Fogg observes, people tend to be "cognitive misers," relying on superficial cues whenever they can get away with it. It's only when a question is personally important to us—when we're concerned about a health problem or contemplating a major purchase—that we're motivated to dig deeper. But that's reason enough for making sure that people know where to start looking.

LETTING THE NET SPEAK FOR ITSELF

San Jose Mercury News, April 17, 2005

———

Summoning the operatic indignation to which only the French language can give full expression, Jean-Noël Jeanneney, the director of the French national library, touched off a national debate not long ago when he said that Google's plans to digitize the collections of major American and British libraries raise "the risk of a crushing American domination in defining the idea of the world that will be held by future generations."

Not that Google's virtual library won't be a boon to humanity, Jeanneney said. But its selection criteria will be "strongly marked by an Anglo-Saxon point of view." It would be "deleterious and detestable," he added, if someone surfing the Web for information about the French Revolution could find nothing but British and American accounts that depict "valiant British aristocrats triumphing over bloodthirsty Jacobins as the guillotine eclipses the Rights of Man."

In the wake of Jeanneney's remarks, commentators warned that French culture was at risk of being marginalized by the process of "omnigooglization." A few weeks ago, President

Jacques Chirac responded to Jeanneney's appeal for a French "counterattack" by asking the national library to draw up plans to accelerate the digitization of its collections, and to work with other European nations to put their libraries online.

Martial metaphors aside, that's welcome news for all *devotés* of French culture and literature, who will have online access, not just to Dickens's and Carlyle's versions of the French Revolution, but also to the French side of the story, as told by Victor Hugo, or better yet, by Alexis de Tocqueville and Jules Michelet.

But the fact that the decision came as a response to the "American challenge" demonstrates how the Web has aggravated concerns about the linguistic and cultural domination of English—and not just among the French. At a conference in Geneva, Switzerland, last year, UN Secretary-General Kofi Annan warned that the predominance of English on the Web was "crowding out voices and views."

That's literally nonsense, of course—on the infinitely extensible Web, nothing can ever be "crowded out." But Annan was giving voice to an impression that's widespread in large parts of the world. And curiously, these concerns seem to be mounting even as the Web becomes less and less of an English lake. The internet was basically a North American development, and the vast majority of its early users was drawn from the United States and the rest of the English-speaking world. But native English speakers now constitute a minority of people using the Web. The proportion of non-English content also is increasing sharply as American internet penetration approaches saturation and as the rest of the world comes online.

In 1997, the linguist Hinrich Schütze and I calculated that about 85 percent of Web pages were in English. Five years later, a study by the Online Computer Library Center came up with a figure of 72 percent. By now the figure is probably under 50 percent, and shrinking rapidly. It's true that many sites in non–English-speaking nations continue to use English to reach an international audience, but the proportion of such sites is dropping as internet use spreads to individuals and small businesses. Nowadays speakers of French and German—or for that matter, of Czech and Hungarian—can accomplish virtually everything they have to without ever needing to visit English-language pages.

Why the continuing concern about English "crowding out" content in other languages, then? One factor may be the search engines, which show the totality of sites from all over the world and often give higher rankings to the more popular English-language pages that are widely linked to. Do an unrestricted Google search on the name of the French writer Roland Barthes, for example, and forty-four of the first fifty sites that come up are in English, with four in French and one each in Spanish and German. The prevalence of English pages among those results may be disconcerting to a Parisian who is accustomed to browsing the reassuringly francophone shelves of the bookstores in the Rue des Écoles. As it happens, though, the ratio is roughly consistent with the numerical proportions of English- and French-speaking internet users—all it shows is that Barthes is held in equal esteem in both communities. And a search on Barthes restricted to French-language pages still turns up seventy-five thousand hits, enough to keep anyone busy for a while.

Rather than decrying omnigooglization, the French and other language communities should welcome it as a sign that distance is no longer an impediment to diffusing information. In the world of print or broadcast, for example, only American news media can achieve anything like worldwide distribution. An American in Strasbourg can easily find CNN or *Time* or the *International Herald Tribune*, but a French speaker has to dig hard to find similar French media in Milwaukee. And for speakers of smaller national languages like Greek or Hungarian, the circulation of information has pretty much stopped at the national borders. Now, however, speakers of those languages can have access to news and opinion in their own languages wherever they happen to be—already a significant factor in communities with large international diasporas that have been historically shut out of their home countries' political discussions.

Even Yiddish has experienced a modest boom in the discussion groups of the Net. One linguist who up to now has spoken Yiddish only with her parents and their friends tells me that for the first time, she can have Yiddish conversations that don't involve the merits of denture creams and early-bird specials.

In the near future, the leveling effect of the internet will extend further. Even if a new film by the French director Olivier Assayas doesn't get extensive international distribution, cinephiles in Cleveland and Caracas will be able to order or download it directly. And the continued digitization of library collections means that those who speak French, German, Japanese, or Hungarian will have access to the literatures of those languages, wherever they happen to be.

But if the internet levels the playing field between English and the other languages of the developed world, it also increases the inequalities between those languages and ones spoken in poor and developing nations, where online access is restricted to a small elite and where even basic information is not available online in the local languages. The digital divide we should all be worrying about is the one between north and south, not the one that runs under the English Channel.

THE AGE OF VALENTINES

Fresh Air Commentary, February 14, 2007

It can take people a while to grasp the implications of a new communications system. When Thomas Edison invented his improved telephone receiver in 1877, he thought it would become a medium for broadcasting concerts and plays to remote auditoriums. For twenty-five years after radio was developed at the end of the nineteenth century, people chiefly regarded it as a means of ship-to-shore communication.

Then there's the US Postal System. For the first half century after its founding, its main function was to circulate newspapers to a national audience. Not that you couldn't send letters, too, but the rates were much higher than for periodicals. In 1840, sending a letter from Boston to Richmond cost 25 cents a sheet, at a time when the average laborer made 75 cents a day. Postal inspectors were always on the alert for people who sent each other newspapers at the cheaper rate and added coded personal messages by putting pin pricks in certain letters.

That all changed in 1845, when Congress enacted the first in a series of laws that sharply reduced the cost of sending letters.

The new rates led to a vast surge in personal correspondence and set up a communications revolution that the historian David Henkin has chronicled in a fascinating new book called *The Postal Age.*

One dramatic effect of the cheaper postage was to allow Americans to keep in touch with one another in what was becoming the most mobile society on earth. But as Henkin recounts, the post was used for other purposes. Businesses made mass mailings of circulars, and swindlers sent out letters promoting get-rich-quick schemes. People sent each other portraits of themselves made with the recently invented daguerreotype process. They sent seeds and sprigs to distant friends and family eager for the smells of home. And, oh yes, they also sent valentines.

St. Valentine's Day was an ancient European holiday. Back in England, people drew lots to divine their future mates and exchanged love poems and intricately folded pieces of paper called "puzzle purses," the ancestors of the fortune-telling cootie-catchers that children still make today. But before the 1840s, puritan Americans almost completely disregarded the holiday, like the other saints' days of the Old World.

The drop in postal rates set off what contemporaries described as "Valentine mania." By the late 1850s, Americans were buying 3 million ready-made valentines every year, paying anything from a penny to several hundred dollars for elaborate affairs adorned with gold rings or precious stones. People sent cards to numerous objects of their affection, often taking advantage of the possibilities for anonymity that the mail provided.

That was alarming to moralists who complained that the postal system in general promoted promiscuity, illicit assignations, and the distribution of pornography—and actually, they weren't entirely wrong about any of that. But fully half of the valentine traffic consisted of comic or insulting cards that people sent anonymously to annoying neighbors or unpopular schoolmasters. By the time the craze tapered off a few decades later, people were sending each other cards for Christmas, Easter, and birthdays, as the greeting card became a fixture of American life.

In a lot of ways, the development of email has followed the same course that the postal system did. For one thing, the implications of the new system weren't clearly understood at first—the first email software was originally designed for transferring files and programs over a network. And once email and other forms of electronic communication became widely available to the public, they were rapidly adapted to almost all the purposes that cheap mail had served. They ushered in a new age of personal communication, but they also facilitated swindles, junk mail, pornography, and anonymous hook-ups and erotic connections. In short, email is used for everything that delighted and troubled observers of the postal system in the mid-nineteenth century.

But following on the heels of cheap long-distance rates, email put the final kibosh on the personal letter. Nowadays, the only personal messages that most people will regularly go to the trouble of putting in the post are the ones that serve a ritual function, like thank-you notes, letters of condolence, or greeting cards. True, you can send a valentine electronically, and some sites will even let you do it anonymously, though you might want to think long and hard about plighting your troth to anybody who's stupid enough to open the attachment on an anonymous email. But for most of us, those kinds of messages can't do their magical work if they don't physically originate with the sender. It's like getting an electronic postcard from friends who are visiting Turkey—it may be nice to hear from them, but you're not going to print it out and stick it on your refrigerator door.

Those remaining postal rituals are a vestigial sign of the allure that letters once exerted on the American imagination. In fact *letter* is about the only word for correspondence that has resisted digitization. We talk about email and electronic notes and messages, but sending a letter still means putting a piece of paper in an envelope. It's true that nowadays the only pieces of paper we can expect to find in our mailboxes that bear a handwritten signature were generally printed by Hallmark. But maybe it's appropriate that the cards that signaled the opening of the postal age should be among its last remnants as it draws to a close.

A WIKI'S AS GOOD AS A NOD

Fresh Air Commentary, June 5, 2006

―――――

If defenders of traditional print culture were looking for a portent that end times are upon us, they might have found it in a sentence from one of Paul Krugman's *New York Times* columns a couple of months ago. The sentence began: "A conspiracy theory, says Wikipedia, 'attempts to explain the cause of an event as a secret, and often deceptive, plot by a covert alliance.'" It was the phrase "says Wikipedia" that had me doing a double take. We usually reserve that kind of attribution for sources that have acquired an institutional voice that transcends their individual contributors. As in, "According to the *Oxford English Dictionary* . . ." or "In the words of the *Encyclopedia Britannica*. . . ." Or for that matter, "the *New York Times* says. . . ." But it was odd to see that lofty syntax used to talk about Wikipedia. It was like quoting some anonymous graffiti written on a bathroom wall in Nassau Hall and prefacing it with, "According to Princeton University. . . ."

But maybe Krugman was just owning up to what most journalists and scholars regard as a guilty secret, which is that they rely on Wikipedia all the time. By "rely on," I don't mean just for doing "preliminary research," which is how academics always say they use Wikipedia, in the same tone that they adopt when they cop to glancing at *People* in the dentist's waiting room. I mean using Wikipedia as a primary source of information.

Or at least I do. In fact I've been keeping a log of the questions I've gone to Wikipedia with in the last few months. Which Edsel models were full-size cars? When did Henry A. Wallace deliver his "Century of the Common Man" speech? What's the difference between discrete and continuous probability distributions? What was the deal with the Nueva Trova movement in Cuban music? And that's not to mention all the names I looked up from my "whatever happened to" file—Pia Zadora, Chuck Knoblauch, Elian Gonzales, Yma Sumac, Vanilla Ice, Joey Heatherton, and the guys from Humble Pie who weren't Peter Frampton.

I almost never bother to verify the answers. Usually I don't much care—like most people, I suspect, I use Wikipedia for idle ruminating, usually when I ought to be doing something else. Anyway, Wikipedia has as good a chance of being right about most of these items as anybody else does. It isn't likely to lead you astray about probability distributions or when Roberto Clemente was National League MVP or when Phil Collins joined Genesis. There are too many people out there who make it a point of pride to know that stuff. And where else would you go to find out about Harry Potter? I haven't actually read any of the Harry Potter books, but I figure that any group of people who take the collective time and trouble to compile a seven-thousand-word article just on Lord Voldemort have got to know what they're talking about.

But sometimes it's unwise to trust the wisdom of crowds. Wikipedians have trouble fixing the date of Daniel Defoe's birth, listing the titles of Max Beerbohm's works, or getting right what Joyce had to say about Ibsen. And Wikipedia is even more helpless at explaining any of those writers. The collective process isn't going to be able to produce the consistent viewpoint or the engaged tone of voice that criticism requires. In fact the prose of Wikipedia is inexorably drawn to a corporate impersonality—it's the way the English language would talk if it had no place to go home to at night.

Still, I expect most users have a good sense of Wikipedia's strengths and limitations. At their best, the articles are well-organized collections of more-or-less reliable facts; at their worst they're so jumbled and incoherent that factual incorrectness is merely a side issue. That's very often the case when the subject is a sprawling one with no standard principle of organization. Reading the entry on the English language, for example, I think of what the physicist Wolfgang Pauli once said about a paper submitted to a journal: "This isn't right. This isn't even wrong."

But what did we expect? The most exasperating thing about all these arguments about Wikipedia is that everybody seems to assume it's a single entity the way an encyclopedia is. The Wikipedians explain how this open collaborative process is lurching toward a neutral and methodical synthesis of all of human knowledge. The critics charge that it's undermining the conception of expertise and intellectual order that the encyclopedia has embodied since the Enlightenment. But in one form or another, that picture of human knowledge was always a grand illusion, even back when we could believe in the unity of high culture. And by now, the encyclopedia is more of a symbol than a tool. Actually, it's my guess that most of the people who harrumph about how Wikipedia is nothing like an encyclopedia haven't actually opened one for some time.

But then Wikipedia is steeped in exactly the same bookish nostalgia. That's implicit in the name Wikipedia itself and the ferociously oedipal rivalry the Wikipedians feel with the Britannica. And it explains the exaggerated deference that Wikipedians pay to print when they insist that articles be documented by reference to published sources, even though a lot of the books and articles the contributors cite turn out to be no more reliable than Wikipedia itself.

The irony is that Wikipedia actually signals the end of the encyclopedic vision. It's only when you actually try to implement that view of collective knowledge that you realize how fond and delusional it is. One way to get a sense of that is to keep clicking the "random article" link and see what comes up: Valseca (Spanish municipality, population 301); Namco System 86 (arcade game system board); Theodicius (Duke of Spoleto, 763–773); Emerald-bellied Puffleg; "One Step Further" (UK entry in European Song Contest, 1982); Walrus Island (Aleutians, 650 meters long, uninhabited); List of North Dakota Public Service Commissioners; Prayer in LDS Theology and Practice; Dirigo High School (Dixville, Maine); *Duc D'Aquitaine* (sixty-four-gun ship of the line of the French Navy, launched in 1754); KYBA (soft-rock station in Rochester, Minnesota). Not that every one of those articles mightn't be useful to somebody or other, but the idea of the "circle of learning"—*encyclopedia* in Latin, from the Greek—is hard to make sense of when the boundaries of the territory seem so infinitely extensible and when so many people are leaving their footprints in the mud. To be sure, that's actually a fair picture of what human knowledge has always been, but it was never so evident before now. The *Wiki-* part is fine, but if it were up to me, I'd lose the *-pedia.**

---

*Under one or another user name I've made contributions to the Wikipedia articles on pleonasm, estate tax in the United States, Rachel (nineteenth-century French actress), *pinko*, consensus reality, "I Fought the Law," kangaroo court, and Brian Horwitz (San Francisco Giants outfielder), among others. That range is typical of most of the project's frequent contributors; when it comes to the crunch, Wikipedia is a vast experiment in aggregated dilettantism.

ALL THUMBS

Fresh Air Commentary, May 16, 2008

═══

By 1848, the new electric telegraph was already being hailed as a modern marvel that would revolutionize commerce, journalism, and warfare. In that year, a prominent New York attorney and editor named Conrad Swackhamer wrote an article predicting that it would transform the language as well. After all, he noted, the telegraph required above all else that its users be brief and direct. As people got used to sending and receiving telegrams and reading the telegraphed dispatches in the newspapers, they would inevitably cast off the verbosity and complexity of the prevalent English style. The "telegraphic style," as Swackhamer called it, would be "terse, condensed, expressive, sparing of expletives, and utterly ignorant of synonyms" and would propel the English language toward a new standard of perfection.

That was the first time anybody used the word *telegraphic* to describe a style of writing, with the implication that a new communications technology would naturally leave its mark on the language itself. It's an idea that has resurfaced with the appearance of every writing tool from the typewriter to the word processor. And now there's a resurgence of Swackhamerism as the keypad is passed to a new generation, and commentators ponder the deeper linguistic significance of the codes and shortcuts that have evolved around instant messaging and cell-phone texting.

The topic got a lot of media play last month with the release of a study on teens and writing technology sponsored by the College Board and the Pew Research Center. According to the report, more than half of teens say they've sometimes used texting shortcuts in their school writing. The story was a natural for journalists. It combined three themes that have been a staple of feature writing for 150 years: "the language is going to hell in a handbasket"; "you'll never get me onto one of those newfangled things"; and "kids today, I'm here to tell you. . . ."

It wasn't hard to find critics who warned of apocalyptic consequences for the language. James Billington, the Librarian of Congress, said that IM and texting were bringing about "the slow destruction of the basic unit of human thought, the sentence." And the enthusiasts of the new media countered with equally momentous predictions. According to Richard Sterling of the National Commission on Writing, texting will naturally erode the conventions of formal writing—within a few decades we probably won't be capitalizing the first words of sentences anymore. In response to that prediction, the *Boston Globe* published an editorial called "the revenge of e. e. cummings" that had no capital letters and was laced with LOLs and texting abbreviations. It had me wondering which is more embarrassing, hearing old people use teenage slang or hearing them make fun of it.

I've got a little prediction to make myself: a generation from now all this stuff is going to sound awfully silly. Did people really imagine that rules of written English sentence structure that go back to the Renaissance would suddenly crumble because teenagers took to texting each other over their cell phones instead of passing notes under their desks in class?

In fact, apart from contributing some slang and jargon, new writing technologies rarely have much of an effect on the language. They can give rise to specialized codes, but those tend to flow alongside the broad channel of standard English without ever mixing with it. As Conrad Swackhamer predicted, the Victorians developed a breathlessly compressed style for sending telegrams, like the message Henry James had one of his characters cable in *Portrait of a Lady*: "Tired America, hot weather awful, return England with niece, first steamer decent cabin." But that telegraphic style didn't leave any traces on Victorian prose—when you think of James's own writing, *terse* and *condensed* are not the words that come to mind.

The linguistic features of the new media are sure to follow the same pattern. Take emoticons. Used sparingly, they can delicately shade the reception of an email—my dean at Berkeley is a master of the deft smiley that turneth away wrath. But it will be a cold day at the copy desk before you encounter a smiley in the pages of the *Economist* or the *New York Review of Books*. What happens in email stays in email.

Kids catch on to this quickly. They may sometimes let texting shortcuts slip into their schoolwork, but they know there are different rules for formal writing, and that you ignore them at your peril. The people at the College Board report they almost never see students using the shortcuts in their SAT essays.

In fact that Pew study reported that a majority of the kids who use IM and texting don't consider them real "writing" at all. And if you think of writing as an intellectual exercise, they're probably right. You're not going to learn a lot about organizing ideas from punching in text messages against a 160-character limit.

But there's another, more basic idea of writing, as the process of translating your thoughts into automatic manual gestures. And in that sense the new technologies do make a difference. As the telegraph first demonstrated, the wonder of modern writing tools is how they can accelerate that process until it seems almost instantaneous—they turn writing into the cognitive equivalent of a twitch game like Pac Man or Tetris. But even with the typewriter and email, the process required all our attention and focus. It's only now that people can do it with a single thumb in the midst of whatever else they happen to be doing, without even having to take their eyes from the blackboard.

SYMBOLS

"VALUES" PLAY

Fresh Air Commentary, July 19, 2004

With the presidential election looking as if it will depend on the votes of nine welders in Cleveland, it was pretty much inevitable that the v-word would rear its head sooner or later. Out on the hustings last week, President Bush said that Senator Kerry is "out of step with the mainstream values that are so important to our country." Meanwhile Kerry was reminding voters of the importance of "relying on the values that made this country great."

A foreigner listening to those claims might think that this election was simply a question of who has better values, like Wal-Mart versus Costco. But it goes deeper than that—it's really about what the word *values* means, and what role it should play in political life.

Values is a word that's made for political mischief, as it slithers from one meaning to another. Sometimes it simply refers to the cultural preferences or mores associated with one group or another, and sometimes it suggests religious principles or morals, the sorts of things that some people have more of than others do. Or often it blends mores and morals together. That distinction was deftly highlighted in a line from the recent movie *Win a Date with Tad Hamilton*. Nathan Lane plays a Hollywood agent who's trying to persuade his dissolute movie star client to dump the small-town West Virginia girl he's smitten with. "Your values are different," Lane tells the actor. "For instance, she has them."

Actually, you could say the same thing about conservatives and liberals. Their values are different; for instance, conservatives have them. At least that's the conclusion you'd reach if you went only by the way *values* is used in the press. Even in the political coverage of supposedly liberal papers like the *New York Times* and the *Washington Post*, the phrase *conservative values* is four times as frequent as "liberal values" is.

But *values* hasn't always been the property of the right. Like that other modern buzzword *community*, it began its life a hundred years ago as a translation of a term from German sociology. And it didn't really enter the general American vocabulary until the 1950s, when it was picked up in progressive circles along with other social-science terms like *alienation* and *peer group*. In those days a sentence like *I share your values* was the sort of thing you'd expect to encounter in a Jules Feiffer cartoon or a Nichols and May routine. The political connotations of *values* were limited to a vague association with progressive education and liberal anticommunism. Back in the '50s a lot of universities were setting up chairs and interdisciplinary programs in *American values*, where the phrase suggested only the democratic ideals that made America different from totalitarian regimes.

It wasn't until the Vietnam era that Republicans seized on *values* as a convenient word for contrasting the mores of middle America with the alarming antics of the hippies and anti-war protesters and the effete pretensions of the East Coast liberal elites. You could date that shift in meaning from August 7, 1968, when the Republicans opened their national convention in Miami Beach with a round of inspirational songs from the preternaturally clean-cut Up with People chorus—"not a hippie among them," as the speaker who introduced them said. Over the next few years, that newly divisive sense of *values* was tirelessly promoted by Vice President Spiro Agnew, the Johnny Appleseed of the culture wars.

From then on, *values* was the word you used to turn every election into a referendum on lifestyles. By 1988, George H. W. Bush could make *values* a literal mantra of his presidential campaign: "I represent the . . . mainstream views and the mainstream values. And they are your values, and my values, and the values of the vast majority of the American people."

By now, in fact, adjectives like *mainstream* and *traditional* aren't really necessary—the bare word *values* alone evokes all those hot-button cultural issues that are summed up as "God, guns, and gays." During last fall's Democratic primaries, Joe Lieberman could say, "[the Republicans] can't say I'm weak on values," and everybody understood that he was talking about his religious convictions and his campaign against sex and violence in the media, not his views on Enron, the environment, or the Iraq war. And when you run into an organization with a name like the American Values Coalition or the Institute for American Values, you can be confident that the American values in question aren't things like "different strokes for different folks" or "a fair day's pay for a day's work"—or for that matter, "pick up after yourself," which is how my mother used to sum up her position on environmental policy.

This time around, the Democrats have made it clear that they're not going to cede the v-word to the Republicans. But when Kerry and Edwards baptized their campaign a "celebration of American values," they weren't referring to the issues on the Republicans' hit list—for them, *values* doesn't have a lot to do with what Howard Stern can say on the radio. As Edwards puts it, values are a matter of "faith, family, opportunity, responsibility, trying to make sure that everybody gets a chance to do what they're capable of doing."

That's a notion of *values* that would have been more familiar to Dwight Eisenhower than to Spiro Agnew—a word for the beliefs we have in common, rather than the ones that divide us. Except that by now the word *values* has been so polemicized that it can't help but suggest an implicit challenge—"You want values? We'll give you values." It says something about what we've come to that a word that ought to be a bland political bromide has turned into a battle cry for both sides.

TEST OF FAITH

New York Times, December 26, 2004

===

In the language of politics, this is a new age of faith. A generation ago, the administration's proposal to allow religious chari-
ties to share in federal funding would have been called the
religion-based initiative, which is how some newspapers with
secular compunctions prefer to describe it even now. But the administration's *faith-based* adds theological undertones—it blends
the notions of religion, as in *the Jewish faith*, and of revealed truth,
as in *faith-based* theories of evolution.

Or take *people of faith*. For most of the twentieth century,
that was merely a pulpity locution reserved for sermons and
commencement addresses, and often with no particular religious force. "I salute you as people of faith, vigor, virility, and
intelligence," Columbia University's president Dwight D. Eisenhower told graduates in 1950.

But the phrase entered a new dispensation in the late 1970s,
when people started to talk about *people of faith* as an alternative to *churchgoers* or *religious practitioners*. The phrase originally

reflected a New Age aversion to identifying with organized religions, but it soon caught on among conservative Christians as well. By now, *people of faith* is ten times as frequent in the press as it was at the beginning of Ronald Reagan's first term. And *of faith* has been transformed into a suffix of its own, as in journalists of faith, physicians of faith, Texans of faith, and pet owners of faith.

That pattern tracks the development of *of color* after *people of color* was revived in the 1970s as a new, inclusive term for nonwhites. And *people of faith* seems to serve a similar function, agglomerating believers of disparate religions into a single political constituency.

That's why *of faith* is reserved for domestic use. *Americans of faith* gets over sixty-two thousand hits on Google, but *Frenchmen of faith*, *Englishmen of faith*, and *Arabs of faith* get none at all. Foreigners can be described as "believers" or "the faithful," even when their religious views draw them to violence or terrorism. But you don't get to put a "person of faith" button on your lapel unless you're eligible to pin an "I voted" button next to it.

The connection to *people of color* isn't accidental: leaders of the Christian right began to speak of "people of faith" around the same time they began to compare their cause to the civil rights movement and to complain about "anti-Christian bias" in the media and the school curriculum. The president echoed that language when he outlined his initiative in 2001: "When people of faith provide social services, we will not discriminate against them."

In his official pronouncements, of course, Bush is careful to define *people of faith* very broadly. Groups shouldn't be denied federal grants, the president said, "just because they have a cross or a Star of David or a crescent on the wall."

But for many, *people of faith* is merely an ecumenical-sounding way of referring to Christian conservatives. Neither crescents nor Stars of David are in evidence at peopleoffaith.com, a site aimed at promoting Christian family values and breaking "the stranglehold of liberal media." And on the day after the election, the Reverend Jerry Falwell boasted that "25 million people of faith" had turned out at the polls, "primarily evangelicals."

Karl Rove uses the term in the same way Falwell does. Asked by the *Christian Science Monitor* if the Republicans had accomplished their goal of turning out an additional 4 million evangelicals, he replied, "I would make it broader, I would make it people of faith. Remember, we gained 5 points among Catholics. It is more than evangelicals and fundamentalists and Charismatics and Pentecostals." But the people of faith in Rove's target market presumably didn't include Los Angeles Jews, Dearborn Muslims, or New England Unitarians, or for that matter People of Faith for John Kerry or Bisexual People of Faith.

The ambiguity of the phrase leaves Bush walking a delicate semantic line. At his press conference following the election, a reporter asked him to comment on his "strong support from people of faith, in particular Christian evangelicals and Pentecostals." Bush answered noncommittally. "I am glad people of faith voted in this election. I appreciate all people who voted," he said and went on to praise American religious pluralism. But despite those public assurances, Bush is obviously aware how Rove uses *people of faith*, and he knows that evangelicals and others are likely to hear his own use of the phrase as a nod to their interests.

Whatever pretence we make of defining *people of faith* in an ecumenical and secular way, we can't ignore the sectarian clouds it trails behind it. For many believers, after all, *faith* is a defining term that always evokes a contrast with faithlessness and apostasy. No one draws an explicit contrast with "people of no faith," but then that isn't necessary to make the point.

The University of California anthropologist Susan Harding, author of *The Book of Jerry Falwell: Fundamentalist Language and Politics*, notes that "when Christian conservatives say 'faith,' they mean 'truth.'" That's fair enough: as Paul puts in the version of Hebrews 11:1 that's preferred by many evangelicals, faith is "the conviction of things not seen." But in that case, maybe we'd do better to talk about "people who believe in the unseen"— or "believers" for short—which would invite less bad faith on all sides.

A DUCK BY ANY OTHER NAME

Los Angeles Times, April 10, 2005

———

There has never been an age as wary as ours of the tricks words can play, obscuring distinctions and smoothing over the corrugations of the actual world. That wariness is implicit in the way we describe words as labels. Not all of them, of course. Nobody would say that *duck* is a label for a kind of waterfowl— *duck* is just the name of the bird. We tend to reserve *label* for social classifications like *fascist, depressive,* or *delinquent,* always with the implication that the word is either misleading and reductive (the labels we describe as "mere") or, at best, a convenience (the ones we describe as "handy"). One way or the other, though, calling a word a label leaves us free to reject it. People say, "I don't believe in labels," but nobody ever says, "I don't believe in names."

Yet as advertisers and marketers know, our mistrust of words doesn't inoculate us against them. We may think of language as an arbitrary system of classification, sewing its seams helter-skelter across the undifferentiated kapok of experience. But we can't help reifying the categories language carves out. The words we dismiss as labels can still exalt or disturb us, which is why we're always having to rationalize away the dissonance, like the shopper who justifies paying a 500 percent premium for a tote bag with a Fendi logo on the grounds you get a better grade of vinyl.

It's hard to think of any words that justify the "label" label more than *liberal* and *conservative*. No one would deny their usefulness as approximate handles: "Liberals have been critical of the Patriot Act." "Conservatives are going to bat for DeLay." But it often seems as if they serve more to pigeonhole than to explain.

Certainly the categories are anything but eternal. It was only during Franklin D. Roosevelt's second term that *liberal* and *conservative* emerged out of a welter of competing terms to become the defining opposition of American politics. To Roosevelt, liberals and conservatives represented "two schools of political belief" about how active a role government should take in fixing problems "beyond the power of men and women to meet as individuals."

A lot of people still see that as the core distinction. But the implications of both terms are different from what they were in Roosevelt's day. In light of recent headlines, it's almost quaint to recall that conservatism used to be associated with isolationism and states' rights. And nowadays both words imply positions on a welter of cultural issues that don't seem "political" in Roosevelt's sense of the term. Few people justify their views on abortion, evolution, or gay marriage by appealing to their philosophy of government—indeed, those positions are often an embarrassment to it.

More important still, we no longer think of liberals and conservatives merely as adherents of different "schools of political belief," in the way we might talk about devotees of supply-side and demand-side as disciples of two economic schools. Now the categories go much deeper—to lifestyle, values, and even traits of character.

The shift in perceptions began with the onset of the culture wars in the 1970s, when the right began to depict liberals as elitists out of touch with "mainstream values." That was also when consumer preferences started standing in for ideological characterizations. Liberals were tarred in a kind of guilt by brand association, as Volvo-driving, brie-eating, Chardonnay-sipping snobs—the "libs," as Rush Limbaugh calls them.

Those stereotypes may not be accurate (as it happens, Republicans buy more brie than Democrats and Volvo-owners split down the middle politically), but they succeed in turning *liberal* into shorthand for a self-indulgent yuppie attitude. Nowadays, the media almost never use phrases like *working-class liberal*—working-class Americans are disqualified from being liberals not because of their political views but because they can't afford the lifestyle.

By now, people talk about liberals and conservatives almost as if they were distinct genders. "You liberals!" a talk-show host will say, in the tone of winking exasperation that recalls "You gals!" And no one sees anything odd when a right-wing commentator publishes a book with the you-just-don't-understand title of *How to Talk to a Liberal (If You Must)*.

Liberals have responded with their stereotypes of the right, as ill-dressed ignorant yahoos from the boonies. (When the

Republican National Convention descended on New York last year, *New York* magazine offered tips to women conventioneers on where to buy coordinated skirt suits and high-end hair spray.) *Red state* and *blue state* have been turned into the names of market segments. A recent article in *Brandweek* reports that Scotts is introducing a new fertilizer aimed at the blue-state market, and *Advertising Age* describes Maxwell House's efforts to "make the blue can a badge of the red states, to make coffee selection a battlefront in the culture wars." And a few months ago, Hardee's CEO defended the restaurant's 1,400-calorie Monster Thickburger as "not a burger for tree-huggers."

For some, the difference goes even deeper than that. In his recent best seller *Don't Think of an Elephant*, Berkeley linguist George Lakoff argues that liberals and conservatives are divided by two different models of the family, the "strict father" family and the "nurturant parent" family. That basic distinction, he says, shapes the differences in opinion on everything from tort reform to same-sex marriage to school vouchers to drilling in the Arctic National Wildlife Refuge.

Lakoff is an astute observer, but in locating the roots of the liberal-conservative distinction in people's basic conceptions of the family, he too is turning the words into something much deeper than "mere labels." As he tells the story, *liberal* and *conservative* go clear to the bone.

Objectively speaking, that picture is hard to defend, not just historically but in light of the way people think about ideological differences in other nations. You can identify groups in British politics that correspond to lowercase liberals and conservatives in Roosevelt's sense of the terms, even if the British don't use the words that way. But the differences don't spill over to cultural issues, and the British are mystified at the way Americans identify ideological affiliations with preferences. During the 2004 Democratic primary season, the London *Daily Telegraph*'s Alec Russell expressed some puzzlement over the political significance attached to the Volvo: "Could this be the first election swung by the Volvo, or rather anti-Volvo, vote? You may think of the Swedish car as a symbol of country tranquility, but in America it is a raging term of abuse."

And the neat dualisms of US politics seem simply irrelevant to nations with no history of a two-party system. For them— and for us, when you come down to it—it makes more sense to identify people in terms of the old spectrum of left and right, which nobody takes as anything more than a seating plan.

But reifications have a way of being self-fulfilling. Nowadays, we can't identify ourselves as liberals or conservatives without making a social identification in the bargain—we imply something about what we drive, whom we're willing to date, and whether we believe in spanking our children. Yet most of us are also aware of just how contingent and historically determined all those connections are.

That's a chronic modern dilemma. No one can live in a state of detachment from language. The trick is to accept a kind of cognitive dissonance about labels, discounting their correspondence to reality even as we realize how persuasive they can be, and making a point never to preface *label* with the self-deluding *mere*.

MAKE OUR BED, AND WE'LL SAY OUR GRACE

Fresh Air Commentary, May 15, 2006

━━━━━

On May 8, 1905, the German-American community of New York commemorated the centenary of the death of the poet Friedrich Schiller. Twenty-five brass bands and six thousand marchers carrying torches and banners paraded up Fifth Avenue, after which more than a thousand celebrants repaired to a *Kommers*, or beer party, where they sang "The Star-Spangled Banner" in German.

As best I can tell from the press reports of the event, nobody thought to be offended by that rendition. Nor did anybody discern a threat to American unity when the German version was sung at events in Baltimore, Sheboygan, and Indianapolis, or when other immigrants sang the anthem in Italian and Czech. In 1901, a former Spanish consul from Chicago personally presented President McKinley with a Spanish translation for use in the newly acquired dependencies of Puerto Rico and the Philippines.

Immigrants were enthusiastic champions of "The Star-Spangled Banner," at a time when it was still vying with other songs to be named the nation's official anthem. The Germans disliked "My Country 'Tis of Thee," which was the other front-runner, because its tune was lifted from "God Save the Queen." And Catholic immigrants objected to the bit about "land of the Pilgrims' pride," which they saw as an allusion to the country's Protestant roots.

The Germans' zest for singing "The Star-Spangled Banner" in their own language wasn't squelched until the First World War, when patriotic fervor led states to pass laws aimed at restricting the use of German. By 1917, nativist groups like the American Rights Committee were denouncing the performance of the anthem in the language of a nation with whom the United States was at war. But even then, people continued to sing the song in other languages—when an Italian version was performed at a Carnegie Hall concert in 1919, the *New York Times* reported that it brought the audience to its feet.

But a lot of modern Americans seemed less appreciative of the tribute when a Spanish-language version of "The Star-Spangled Banner" called "Nuestro Himno" was released last month. Some took the translation as a sign that immigrants were refusing to learn English. President Bush said, "I think people who want to be a citizen of this country ought to learn English, and they ought to learn to sing the national anthem in English." The conservative commentator Michelle Malkin described the song as "the illegal alien national anthem" and asked indignantly, "Who's assimilating whom?" Even some supporters of the immigrant groups saw the song as a declaration of linguistic independence. The Chilean playwright Ariel Dorfman wrote defiantly that the song signaled that America is "on its way to becoming a bilingual nation" that will "soon be articulating its identity in two languages."

What's the Spanish for *poppycock?** The fact is that the vast majority of Hispanics in America already speak English, and the rest are learning it much faster than the Germans, Italians, or those Norwegian bachelor farmers did a century ago. Back then, after all, the economic incentives for learning English were nowhere near as great as they are now. Most immigrants lived in isolated rural areas or urban ethnic enclaves, and a lot of cities had separate school systems for immigrants—in 1900, there were more than six hundred thousand children doing all or most of their primary instruction in German.

According to demographers, the average immigrant family in 1900 took more than three generations to make the transition to English dominance—now it takes just over two. By the third or fourth generation, in fact, most American Hispanics are as depressingly monolingual in English as any other American group.

But in the meantime, Americans are uneasy with the idea that anyone can serve two linguistic masters. Everybody pays tribute to our magnificent diversity, of course. But like everything else in America, diversity has gotten pretty uniform these days—you think of an airport food court where Taco Bell is nestled between Noah's Bagels and Pizza Hut.

And the anxiety about multilingualism is amplified by a consumer culture that makes the phenomenon more visible nationally than it used to be, even if foreign-language speakers are actually a smaller proportion of the population than they were

---

*The *Oxford Spanish-English Dictionary* suggests *paparruchas*, which has just the right old-fashioned tone. But depending on the dialect and register, the claims that Hispanics are not learning English could also be fairly described as *tonterías, gillopolleces, chorradas, pavadas, bobadas, sandeces, estupideces, macanas,* or *pendejadas.* It's a language that can go English *palabra-a-palabra* in words for claptrap.

in Teddy Roosevelt's time. It isn't just all the media flap surrounding the anthem. People feel a swell of indignation when they encounter other languages on billboards or ATMs, or as they're spinning their radio dials. Once you let these people have their way on Burger King menus, how far could it be to ethnic separatism and civil war?

Those were the specters that Senator Lamar Alexander evoked when he introduced a Senate resolution earlier this month that affirms that the anthem should be sung only in English. "Jerusalem is diverse," he said. "The Balkans are diverse. Iraq is diverse."

Well, but then so is my neighborhood of San Francisco, but we don't have any car bombs going off just yet. I wonder if Alexander would have been reassured by an article by Ann Powers that appeared in the *Los Angeles Times* last week. Powers noted that the real anthem of the new immigrant movement isn't "Nuestro Himno" or Ricardo Arjona's haunting "Mojado" (or "Wetback"). It's Neil Diamond's gloriously hokey "They're Coming to America," which the singer originally wrote as a tribute to his own immigrant grandparents. Latinos picked up on the song twenty years ago, when Cheech Marin used it in his movie *Born in East L.A.*, and it has been played at immigrants' rights rallies from Los Angeles to Kansas City and Milwaukee.

Now there's an image that Lou Dobbs could keep people up nights with. Millions of brown-skinned aliens pouring over our borders—singing *Neil Diamond songs*!

THIS ISN'T PATRIOTISM

Los Angeles Times, September 9, 2006

"We were not Democrat or Republican on that horrible day. We were not liberal or conservative. We were Americans, by God!" As it happens, those sentences appeared in the *San Diego Union-Tribune* on September 13, 2001, but you encountered the same sentiment everywhere you looked in the days and weeks after 9/11.

For a moment, it really did look as if everything was going to be different. "Sept. 11 made it safe for liberals to be patriots," George Packer wrote in the *New York Times*, as many liberals found themselves hanging flags and making other unfamiliar gestures.

Thoughtful liberals denounced the "one-eyed left," as Todd Gitlin described them, who called the attacks payback for American crimes. Thoughtful conservatives recoiled when Jerry Falwell and Pat Robertson said that the attacks were God's punishment on abortionists, feminists, gays, and the ACLU.

It couldn't have lasted. "America Unites," read the banner at Fox News in the days after the attack, but what it really meant was "Welcome aboard." For the last thirty years, after all, conservatives have treated patriotism as their own gated community.

Patriotic liberal may not be an oxymoron, exactly, but it's an unexpected collocation, like *dour Neopolitan*. On Google, it's outnumbered by *patriotic conservative* by 20 to 1. So the right took the liberals' tentative displays of patriotic feeling as an admission that they had seen the error of their America-blaming ways—a sign, as David Brooks put it in the *Daily Standard*, that "the most reactionary liberals amongst us are capable of change." Yet liberals were hardly "rediscovering" patriotism; most of them had been deeply devoted to this nation all along. Even before the attacks, a large majority of Democrats described themselves as "very proud" or "extremely proud" to be an American—not quite as many as Republicans, to be sure, but still vastly more than the citizens of long-established nations such as Britain, France, and Japan. Such unanimity isn't the stuff of which wedge issues are made.

But since the Vietnam War era, liberals have been wary about the displays and avowals that have always given American patriotism its singular character. "It is impossible to conceive a more troublesome or more garrulous patriotism; it wearies even those who are disposed to respect it," Alexis de Tocqueville wrote in 1840. And Europeans ever since have marveled at our enthusiasm for showing our flag and expatiating on our national virtues—not just for the edification of foreigners but as a reproach to other Americans whose undemonstrativeness suggests a want of proper patriotic devotion.

It's a curious characteristic of American patriotism, in fact, that most of us think we're more patriotic than the next guy. In surveys, Americans greatly exaggerate the "patriotism gap,"

dramatically underestimating the proportion of their countrymen who say they're extremely patriotic. In a recent Fox
News/Opinion Dynamics poll, two-thirds of us—and 80 percent of Republicans—claim to be more patriotic than the average American. In short, most of us like to think that
patriotism is a lot more exceptional than it actually is.

So it's no wonder that patriotic gestures are so often laced
with partisan belligerence. Wearing an American flag in your
lapel, the *Wall Street Journal*'s Peggy Noonan said approvingly
a few years ago, is "a sign that says 'I support my country, and
if you don't like it, that's too bad.'" And since 9/11, Republicans have taken with high zest to depicting Democrats as lack-
ing in patriotism.

True, Republican elected officials tend to avoid the p-word itself. Sometimes the charge is made obliquely; during the 2004
campaign, Vice President Dick Cheney volunteered on at least
thirty occasions that he wasn't challenging John Kerry's patriotism, often repeating the point so it wouldn't be lost on anybody. But President Bush and other Republican officials have
made the message clear with language like "undermining troops
in the field," "making politics the bottom line in the war on terror," "encouraging our enemies" and the recent "Defeatocrats."
And Republicans have been able to slough off Democratic sug-
gestions that real patriotism might not include passing wartime
tax cuts for the rich or slighting domestic security needs. How
could Republicans be unpatriotic when the rhetoric of patriotism is theirs alone to deploy?

Still, it's striking how formulaic and awkward that rhetoric
is coming to sound. It may be a wholly new type of war that
we're watching on TV, but the score often sounds as if it were

taken from *The Green Berets*—or even from *Watch on the Rhine*, to listen to the administration's recent talk about *fascism* and *appeasers*.

Rhetorical gestures take on new meanings when their connection to reality frays. Rebaptizing sauerkraut as "liberty cabbage" during World War I was a hysterical overreaction to a real enemy; rebaptizing french fries as "freedom fries" during the buildup to the Iraq war was a bratty swipe at an ally with reservations about the Iraq invasion, not to mention at the Roquefort-sniffing "liberal elite" that shared them.

You hear the same disconnect in the way people use *appeaser*, *defeatist*, *aid and comfort*, *America-haters*, and the like. The terms are meant to conjure up the spectral targets of patriotic bile in earlier eras—traitors, fifth columnists, subversives, and radicals who harbored alien allegiances. But it takes a febrile imagination to see those shades in Democrats whose subversiveness is confined to questioning whether throwing more dog tags at Iraq will give terrorists in London or Madrid second thoughts about mounting new attacks.

Political attacks that sounded sinister in the McCarthy years now sound merely outlandish, as conservatives try to explain liberals' lack of patriotism as just another one of those blue-state lifestyle traits, like an aversion to Lynyrd Skynyrd or macaroni and cheese. Writing shortly after the 9/11 attacks, the *National Review*'s John O'Sullivan explained that liberals' anti-Americanism was the reaction of snobs who believed that "the patriotism of ordinary people is something simplistic, vulgar and shameful," which is why liberals are more comfortable taking the side of "medieval Islamists" than of "a hard-hat construction worker or a suburban golfer in plaid pants."

You can't trivialize love of country more than that. If liberals are capable of bailing out on patriotism simply because it's tacky, how strong a hold could it have on any of us? But then patriotism has never been so low-maintenance as now. Time was when "supporting the troops" obliged you to buy war bonds or go out on scrap drives. Now you merely have to slap a bumper sticker on the back of your Hummer. And even for the able-bodied, it's enough to support the troops from afar— you don't see conservative young women out in the streets handing out white feathers as emblems of cowardice to men who aren't in uniform.

The less it costs to proclaim yourself a patriot, the less your political adversaries have to do to be accused of being unpatriotic—it's enough that they question the wisdom of a policy or leave their lapel pins on their other suit. For a moment there, it was going to be different.

CIVILITY WARS

Fresh Air Commentary, September 13, 2007

━━━━━

Sometimes a change in the language reflects a change in the world, sometimes just a change in the way we talk about it. And sometimes it isn't easy to tell.

Civility began its life as a word for citizenship and a close kin of *civilization*. But by the early twentieth century it had dwindled to a genteel term for a nominal courtesy or for perfunctory expressions of politeness—"They exchanged civilities" —the sort of word that transit companies posted on bus placards in those recurring campaigns aimed at getting riders and employees to be nicer to one another.

Back then, people didn't actually talk about *civility* very much—they were much more likely to complain about bad manners, rudeness, or discourtesy. As late as the 1950s, the words *civility* and *incivility* were appearing in the *New York Times* only about five or six times a year. The words didn't take off until the 1960s—in 1969 alone, they appeared in the *Times* more often than they had over the entire eight-year Eisenhower presidency, and by now they're thirty times more common in the media than they were then.

A lot of people would explain that sudden rise in civility talk as a direct response to a breakdown in public manners: in a Public Agenda poll a couple of years ago, three-quarters of the respondents said that Americans used to treat each other with more respect and courtesy in the past. But then every generation since Victorian times has had exactly the same impression. Etiquette writers in the 1920s railed about people who monopolized party lines, rude street-car conductors, women who pushed you out of their way at department stores, hosts who invited you to dinner and then made you listen to their favorite radio programs, and of course the discourteous motorists who were classified as roadster rowdies, coupe cads, and van vandals (out of that bestiary of boors only the road hog has survived).

But to traditionalists, the provocations of the social movements of the '60s seemed to go beyond mere breaches of decorum, or beyond anything that could be conveyed by old words like *impolite*, *rude*, and *discourteous*. So they reached back to reclaim an older sense of *civility*, which invested personal deportment with a layer of civic and political consequence. At the time, it was a self-conscious archaism: writing in 1958, the conservative sociologist Edward Shils deplored the word's loss of political significance: "Civility . . . has been allowed to dwindle to the point where it has come to refer to good manners in face-to-face relationships."

In an editorial that appeared just before the 1968 elections, the *Wall Street Journal* inveighed against what it called the New Incivility. As the *Journal* described them, the culprits included the student protesters, the "filthy hecklers who dogged the steps of presidential candidate Hubert Humphrey," and the "enraged Negro spokesmen" who "denied any virtue in white civilization." And the offense wasn't just in what all the hippies and protesters were saying, but their disagreeable physical appearance—with their slovenly hair, beards, and clothing and their general squalor, the *Journal* said, they were showing their contempt for "the world of decent manners."

As philosophers and sociologists use the word, *civility* is something distinct from simple politeness—more like the attitudes and behavior that make our public discourse possible. But in the mouths of most modern critics, the power of *civility* and *incivility* lies precisely in their ability to blur the lines between personal and public life. *Incivility* seems to draw everything that's coarse, irritating, or merely thoughtless in American daily life into a single great rent in the nation's moral and political fabric. It's hard to think of any other social vice that covers as much ground: cell-phone abuse, brusque store clerks, airlines that keep people sitting on the tarmac for hours, telemarketers, reality TV, email spam, road rage, shock jocks, and nightclub hecklers, not to mention congressional partisanship, attack ads, hostile bloggers, belligerent talk-show hosts, and the people who post abusive comments on blogs and news sites. A recent book on incivility in the workplace uses the word for everything from overuse of the fax machine to excessive use of email acronyms to insisting on a fixed agenda in brainstorming sessions.

There's clearly a lot to get worked up about out there, and *incivility* bundles it all up in a cognitively efficient package. The word by itself does a lot of the work of connecting the contentious tenor of political life to a general decline in personal values. Armed with the notion of incivility, critics can decry the routine crudeness of broadcast expletives, hip-hop lyrics, and gross-out movies like *American Pie* as the harbingers of im-minent social and political disintegration. Chalk it all up to television, secularism, sixties radicalism, permissive parenting, the internet, or according to George Will, to "the dark side of the New Economy," which has "showered sudden wealth on people who behave as badly as the arrivistes in Balzac's novels" and created an e-culture that "glorifies speed over decorum and innovation over tradition."

But the charge of incivility also provides a cover for writing off serious political speech in the same way we dismiss rude-ness and intemperateness in everyday life. Speaking slightingly of the president becomes morally indistinguishable from say-ing nasty things about a coworker in the lunchroom. In the course of things, the charge of incivility can close off serious discussion every bit as effectively as actual rudeness can.

What makes *civility* and *incivility* so usefully elastic is that the words live out their entire existence on op-ed pages, with no grounding in the homey truths of everyday life. Parents don't teach their children about civility and incivility, which are words most people learn only when they're prepping for the vocabulary items on the SATs. They teach them about things like manners, respect, and politeness—those are the real fam-ily values. And while a lot of the forms of behavior that people describe as incivility would count as simple bad manners, many of them wouldn't. When you hear people talk about incivility, it's useful to ask whether a word like *impoliteness* or *rudeness* would have done as well. If so, why didn't they use those words? And if not, what are they trying to put past you?

WHERE THE ELITES MEET

Fresh Air Commentary, April 25, 2008

═══

People are always splitting off new meanings for words. Much more rarely they'll smoosh together two old ones. As with other kinds of inbreeding, the process can produce monsters. Take the curious recent development of the noun *elite*. Not long ago it was a barely nativized French word that still opened with a jaunty *accent aigu* on its *é* (the *New Yorker* still holds the line on that spelling). Now it can drive items like *health care, torture,* and *immigration* to the bottom of a network's debate agenda.

Elite has several traditional meanings. It can be a la-di-da word for the upper crust, what people used to call *the bon ton.* Or more consequentially, it can denote the interlocking command structure of society that the sociologist C. Wright Mills referred to in the title of his classic 1956 book *The Power Elite.* As Mills described them, those were "the people who rule the big corporations . . . run the machinery of the state [and] direct the military establishment."

Until a few decades ago, those senses of *elite* rarely even nodded to each other. The first appeared only in the society pages and the names of pastry shops; the second showed up only in foreign political dispatches and sociology journals. (Of course *elite* is also used as both an adjective and a noun to refer simply to the cream of a class—*elite runners, elite fighting force, the NBA elite*, and so on—where the word has no particular social or political connotations.)

The blurring of the senses of *elite* was first audible in the 1960s, when Spiro Agnew put the phrase *media elite* into wide circulation and joined it with descriptions like *effete snobs*, so as to conflate the social and political meanings of the word. But the new meaning of *elite* didn't really make its debut until the summer of 1992, when Vice President Dan Quayle sparked a national controversy by denouncing Candace Bergen's TV character Murphy Brown for having a child out of wedlock. Quayle put the blame on a "cultural elite" who were mocking ordinary Americans "in newsrooms, sitcom studios, and faculty lounges all over America. . . . We have two cultures," he said, "the cultural elite and the rest of us."

Those attacks weren't sufficient to save the Bush-Quayle ticket from going down in the fall elections, but they did put the e-word at the center of national attention. When he was asked who exactly made up the cultural elite, Quayle answered coyly, "They know who they are." But *Newsweek* obligingly published a list of its hundred most prominent members, which with scrupulous evenhandedness included both poster-child liberals like Bill Moyers, Frank Rich, Susan Sontag, and Oprah and poster-child conservatives like William Bennett, George Will, William Safire, and Lynne Cheney.

By any reasonable standard of cultural influence, those were all uncontroversial calls. But by then, *elite* had been sent spinning inexorably leftwards. It wasn't just that it was now exclusively prefixed by *liberal* and implied a seditious taste in cheese and beverages. Even the job descriptions of the elite had changed, so that the qualifier *cultural* came to seem redundant.

In the British media, you still see *elite* used predominantly to refer to economic and business leaders, whether you look at the left-wing *Guardian* or Rupert Murdoch's *Times* of London. But on Murdoch's Fox News, references to the media elite outnumber references to the business and corporate elite by 40 to 1, and the disproportion is only slightly less dramatic on CNN. When Americans hear *elite* these days, they're less likely to think of the managers and politicians who inhabit the centers of power than of the celebrities, academics, and journalists who lodge in its outer boroughs.

It remained only for *elite* to undergo its final democratization, where it was emptied of its last connections to social position or to actual wealth or power. All that was left of its original meanings was the implication of insufferable pretension and an unwarranted sense of entitlement. As the conservative radio host Laura Ingraham explains it in *Shut Up and Sing*, elite Americans "are defined not so much by class or wealth or position as they are by a *general outlook*. Their core belief is that they are superior to We the People. They think we're stupid. They think where we live is stupid. They think our SUVs are stupid. They think our guns are stupid."*

---

*Ingraham simply calls these people "elites," having adopted the new practice of using *elite* to refer to individuals, as in "Paris Hilton is one of those elites who live on their parents' wealth." The usage sounds weird to my no-doubt-fogeyish ear, but it's distributed democratically across the political spectrum.

That broadened meaning of *elite* is apt to create some confusion for liberals who haven't cottoned to it. They're apt to get indignant when they hear *elite* pronounced with a sneer by people who would indisputably qualify for the label under its old definition. And they may be puzzled by the expansive use of *we* that modern critics of the liberal elite tend to fall into when they're bonding with non-elite Americans. How does a Connecticut-raised, Ivy-educated lawyer like Ingraham get to share a first-person plural pronoun with a working-class deer hunter from western Pennsylvania?

For that matter, what are we supposed to make of that *we* when we hear it from the quintessential blue-state conservative David Brooks? "Is Obama someone who doesn't know anything about the way American people actually live, or does he actually get the way we live?" I mean, if you give Brooks that *we*, who exactly is the *they* supposed to be?

But then if you don't have to have money, power, or influence to qualify as elite, it follows that having those things needn't necessarily disqualify you from being one of the rest of us, so long as you can knock back a shot occasionally and commune with your inner *g*-dropper. The crucial thing, as Barack Obama learned, is not to be caught looking out of touch—a phrase that was paired with his name in 3,500 Google News stories after the "bittergate" episode. Summer wherever you like, but if you don't want to be described as elite, you'd better be able to work Dale Earnhardt Jr. into your conversation.

THE PASSING SCENE

BRANDING THE PHONETOSPHERE

Fresh Air Commentary, September 2, 2004

═══════

Not long ago, a French branding consultant announced that he had done a study that showed that brand names account for two out of five words that the average person knows. I'm a little dubious about that result—it puts me in mind of the well-known fact that 57 percent of all quoted statistics are made up on the spot. But the estimate probably isn't wildly off.

I figure I know twenty or thirty common nouns for kinds of automobiles—convertible, sedan, SUV, hardtop, limo, and so forth. But I know several hundred names of car makes and models. And the proportions are similar for breakfast cereals, soft drinks, and shampoos. Of course the vast majority of those trademarks live in the noun neighborhood of my mental dictionary—the regions inhabited by verbs, adjectives, and prepositions are relatively uncluttered by commercial messages. But the Patent and Trademark Office lists over 4 million terms that someone has tried to trademark at one time or another, and the list is growing by about a hundred thousand a year.

Even if only a tiny fraction of those wind up settling in your brain, they make for a big constituency.

Think of the English language as a vast expanse of words and syllables—what the linguist Geoffrey Pullum calls the phonetosphere. Most of that space has been staked out by private interests now, some of them small homesteaders and some of them great brand barons with thousands of names under their control. It's a territory torn by border wars, particularly as companies extend their brand names into new areas of business, where they may brush up against the similar-sounding brands of competitors. Nowadays, more than 80 percent of new product names are the extensions of established brands. All of a sudden a computer company and a music publisher can be at odds over who has the right to use *apple* for a music download service. And at the center of it all is the patch of free range that we think of as the common language, where words aren't accountable to anyone at all.

The branding people have a complicated relationship to that common language. They're always abducting its inhabitants to serve a single master as a brand or slogan, but they also have an interest in maintaining its neutrality, like a linguistic Switzerland. That isn't just because they need the verbs and prepositions that flourish there, but because they need all those generic phrases like *bathroom tissue* and *plastic wrap* that keep their trademarks from becoming common nouns that anybody could use. Whatever you or I may think, in the minds of trademark attorneys, all brand names are really secret adjectives—not Oreos but "OREO brand sandwich cookies," not Skippy but "SKIPPY brand peanut butter spread."

But trademark holders live in fear of seeing their own brands jump the wall and cast off their capital letters. Over the years, that has been the fate of a lot of trademarked names, like pogo stick, heroin, cellophane, dry ice, leatherette, jungle gym, and zipper. And there are dozens of other trademarks that are clinging to legal life by a thread. Mary Janes and Loafers, Ouija board and Peg-Board, Tabasco sauce and Mini-bar, Skivvies and Sheetrock, Windbreakers and Seeing-Eye dogs, Dumpsters and Dobros—not a lot of people write those words with capital letters, even if every one of them is still legally entitled to the honor.

Dictionaries are supposed to be the guardians of the common language, but they're reluctant to naturalize any of those asylum seekers from brand space. They can ignore the objections of pressure groups when it comes to listing obscenities or ethnic slurs, and they have no compunction about including slang items or malapropisms that set the teeth of the language police on edge. But crossing your own legal department takes a different kind of moxie (another former brand name, by the way). When it comes to defining words that are still trademarked, lexicographers suddenly discover the virtues of discretion. Look up the verb *Xerox* in *Merriam-Webster's*, for example, and you'll see an entry "to make (a copy) on a Xerox copier." As in, "Did you Xerox the documents?" "No, but I Konica'd some and Toshiba'd the rest." It's a definition that clearly had its origin on legal stationery, not in anybody's actual use of the verb.*

---

*Not long after this piece appeared, the Merriam-Webster people changed the definition of the verb to "to copy on a xerographic copier."

Some people find the profusion of brand names alarming—you could have the impression that we're privatizing the language in the same way we're privatizing the national forests. But as the Frenchman who did that study points out, it has a useful side effect. The great brands don't belong to any single language—they're part of a new global tongue, the Esperanto of the checkout stand. You may not know how to say "soft drink" or "athletic shoe" in Italian, but nowadays you can always get by in Rome by asking for a Coca-Cola or Nikes. From an international point of view, those are the real common nouns now. We're all drawn together under the international lingua branda, with only our separate verbs to keep us apart.

WHEN WORDS BREAK DOWN

Fresh Air Commentary, September 8, 2005

━━━━━

The breakdowns in the wake of Hurricane Katrina extended to more than the levees around New Orleans and the local and federal relief efforts. The language seemed to be caving in, too. *Looting, evacuee, act of God*—all of a sudden, the familiar words seemed inadequate to contain the events we were watching.

Take *looting*. Like *thug*, it comes from a Hindi word the British brought back with them from India. (It's striking how many of the words we use for criminality are borrowed from other languages, as if these were alien notions—*marauder* from French, *desperado* from Spanish, *bandit* from Italian, *assassin* from Arabic, *vandal* from the Vandals.)

Time was that *looting* chiefly referred to the pillaging done by troops or bandits. Nowadays it evokes images of mobs of people carting off TV sets as the social order collapses around them.

In the past, though, people gave little thought to the word. Nobody fretted that *looting* might be too simplistic to describe what was going on in the Watts and Newark riots or after the fall of Baghdad. But last week the notion suddenly became problematic. Making off with flat-screen TVs was one thing, but was *looting* the right word for taking diapers and bottled water from a convenience store?

Some hewed to an uncompromising moral absolutism. When the White House press secretary Scott McClellan was asked about people taking necessities in his press briefing on September 1, he defended the president's zero-tolerance policy on looting. Food and water were being sent to the afflicted areas, he said; looting was not the way to obtain them.

But in the light of the news reports that the promised help hadn't been exactly expeditious, even the administration's partisans were willing to make some room for situational ethics. Of course the looters should be shot, the *Wall Street Journal's* Peggy Noonan said. But by looters she meant the people who were taking what they wanted and not simply what they needed.

That was pretty much where people were drawing the moral line, as they waded into all those unforeseen semantic subtleties. You were within your rights to walk out of a supermarket with a loaf of Wonder Bread and a jar of Skippy, but woe betide you if your bag turned out to contain Carr's Water Crackers and a tin of foie gras.

Then too, *looting* seemed to have racial overtones, as if it still bore the traces of its origin in the British Raj. A number of bloggers pointed to two press agency photographs that were posted on Yahoo! News. One showed a young black man carrying a bag of food in chest-deep water with a caption that described him as looting; another showed a fair-skinned couple in identi-

cal circumstances and described them as "finding" food at a local grocery store. Whatever the actual reasons for that difference
in language, the photos reinforced the suspicion that the words
were being used selectively.

Some media tried to simplify the problem by using *looting*
across the board. The *New York Times* ran a story about how the
remaining inhabitants of the unflooded French Quarter were
making a grim party of the crisis, appropriating food and water from local stores. "Don't call it looting, please," one resident
was quoted as saying. But that's exactly what the *Times* did,
probably to forestall the impression that they were giving white
foragers a pass.

Others bailed out on the l-word entirely. The editor of a Wis-
consin newspaper instructed his news desk to replace *looting* with
taking in photo captions. As he put it, "I can't know whether
somebody taking battery-powered tools from a ruined hardware
store is 'looting' or trying to find something he can use to get
grandma out of the attic."

True, *taking, finding*, and *making off* all had a makeshift feel.
But in the circumstances, makeshift seemed appropriate. After
a thousand years of social inequality and natural disasters, the
English language still doesn't have a word for someone who
steals a loaf of bread to feed his family.

A similar problem came up in describing those displaced by
the floods. *Evacuees* brings to mind people who are moved out
of town for a week until a chemical cloud blows away, not a
long-term dislocation. And while *internally displaced persons* is
probably the most accurate term, nobody wants to sound like
a federal bureaucrat right now.

Those difficulties led a lot of broadcasters and journalists to describe the displaced people as refugees. As it happens, that's another borrowed word, from the French name for the Huguenots who went to England when their religious freedom was withdrawn with the revocation of the Edict of Nantes in 1685.

You could argue that there's some precedent for using the word in situations like this one—Woody Guthrie used it in his famous song "Dust Bowl Refugee," when a combination of natural disaster and government inaction led to another massive displacement of poor people in America. .

But to most Americans, *refugee* brings to mind the image of those who are forced to seek asylum in another country because of war, political turmoil, or persecution, which is how most dictionaries and international organizations define the word. Some black leaders objected to those implications—and indeed, it turns out that the press has been using *refugee* disproportionately in the neighborhood of *poor* or *black* or in reference to the people gathered in the Astrodome.

On Tuesday, President Bush said he agreed with them. "The people we're talking about are not refugees," he said. "They are Americans, and they need the help and love and compassion of our fellow citizens."

Some newspapers and wire services have defended the use of *refugee* as meaning simply someone who seeks refuge. But that doesn't seem right—ducking into a ski hut to wait out a blizzard doesn't make me a refugee.

And at a time like this, it's hard to defend a term that some victims of the disaster are likely to be offended by. "It makes me feel like I'm from another country," one survivor in Houston said.

Evacuees, victims, displaced, refugees, survivors—as with the question of what to use in place of *looting* of food and water, there's no ideal solution here. But that's as it should be. If you weren't struggling to find the right language to describe what you were seeing over the last two weeks, you probably weren't paying close enough attention.

AN ADJECTIVE FOR CAKES,
BUT NOT FOR BILL GATES

New York Times, April 30, 2006

━━━━

By any objective standard, there are more rich Americans than ever before. More than 8 million of us are worth more than $1 million, exclusive of our homes, according to one recent estimate. And when it comes to what used to be called serious money, the number of households with assets over $10 million has quintupled since 1980.

Wealth has grown so common that according to a 2003 Gallup poll, half of those under thirty think they'll be rich someday. But *rich* is notoriously a moving target, which always seems to lie just over the financial horizon. The Gallup survey found that those who earned less than $30,000 a year said on average that it would take an income of $74,000 to make them rich, those earning between $30,000 and $50,000 said it would take $100,000, and those earning over $50,000 said they required $200,000. That may explain why despite increasing wealth, the number of Americans who are willing to describe themselves as rich has stayed at 1 to 2 percent over the past twenty years. And fewer than a tenth of those with $1 to 4 million in financial assets are willing to describe themselves as wealthy—the rest opt for "comfortable."

In part, that's because we reckon how rich we are, as Samuel Johnson said, "not by the calls of nature, but by the plenty of others." After all, if you're still flying commercial and your business school classmates have their own Gulfstreams, it's easy to forget that there was a time when your wildest dreams of riches only went as far as a seat in first class.

A few years ago, *Inc.* magazine reported that few of the CEOs of America's fastest-growing private companies considered themselves rich. And even those at the very top of the ladder seem to be sheepish about describing themselves with the r-word. Asked in 2003 if he felt rich, Bill Gates would only concede, "At this point I'm clearly not by some definition middle class."

Unlike *prosperous* or *affluent*, *rich* implies a society divided into separate estates, a legacy of the word's origin in the Indo-European name for a tribal king. People may disagree on exactly how much money it takes to be rich, but that only confirms that it's an absolute threshold, and that those who have crossed it are delivered from the cares that afflict the rest of us. (Nobody who wins the lottery cries, "I'm affluent!")

Those vaguely undemocratic implications are apt to evoke charges of class warfare when politicians refer to the rich. In his 1994 book, *The Agenda*, Bob Woodward reported that Treasury Secretary Robert Rubin, himself a wealthy man, urged President Bill Clinton to speak only of "the well-to-do"—a phrase that suggests a respectably prosperous patent lawyer, not Paris Hilton.

These days, in fact, it's usually only entertainers and celebrities who unapologetically revel in being rich, mindful of their obligation to live out the fantasies of the rest of us. "My God is a God who wants me to have things," Mary J. Blige recently told *Blender* magazine. "He wants me to bling."

Blige would have found many kindred spirits a century ago, when the marks of worldly success were "leisure and a conspicuous consumption of goods," as Thorstein Veblen observed in *The Theory of the Leisure Class*, and when the rich justified their fortunes by the aesthetic opportunities they afforded. "Money's only excuse is to put beauty into circulation," as one of Edith Wharton's characters put it. But the phrase *the idle rich* has vanished since then, along with the bloated top-hatted plutocrats who used to populate editorial cartoons. Today's leaner billionaires claim to desire money not as a means of avoiding work but as proof of how good they are at it. The money, they avow, is merely a way of keeping score.

Today's rich may spend as profusely as the robber barons of the last Gilded Age, but most try to be more circumspect about it, while insisting that they still feel middle-class like everyone else. Indeed, it was the revelations of conspicuous blinging, as much as his legal derelictions, that brought a shower of scorn on the head of the former Tyco chief executive L. Dennis Kozlowski.

Whether it's applied to people or pastries, *rich* still suggests surfeit and unwholesome excess. *Filthy rich*, we say, which is a far cry from *dirt poor*. Hence a paradox. "I want to be rich"— the fantasy of possessing more wealth than anyone could possibly ever need—is the driving force of capitalism. But the very extravagance that *rich* implies ensures that most of those who achieve that dream will feel reluctant to acknowledge it.

LIFESTYLE CHOICE

Fresh Air Commentary, July 31, 2006

———

Some words are born stars, but others have to wait patiently in the wings for years until the world suddenly realizes it has a need for them. *Lifestyle* entered the language in the early twentieth century, but for the first fifty years of its existence, it was an obscure bit of sociological and psychoanalytic jargon. In the whole of 1967, the word appeared in the *Chicago Tribune* exactly 7 times. Within five years that figure had jumped to 3,300, and the word was on everybody's lips. A newspaper cartoon showed a little boy who, coming home from school, tells his mom, "Today we learned about the unalienable rights—lifestyle, liberty, and the pursuit of happiness."

Some of the credit for that surge belongs to a 1970 book by a Yale professor named Charles Reich. *The Greening of America* was an exuberant paean to the youth culture, with its beads, bell-bottoms, drugs, and casual sex. The new lifestyle, Reich said, presaged nothing less than the advent of a new form of human consciousness that would prove to be far more world-shaking than the merely political upheavals like the Russian or French revolutions.

In retrospect, as the *Weekly Standard*'s David Skinner pointed out recently, Reich did little more than raise the modish radical clichés of the era to the status of profundities. The critics on all sides were scathing—liberals panned the book because it suggested that sex and drugs were an alternative to political activism; conservatives panned it because it countenanced sex and drugs at all. Just last year, in fact, the conservative weekly *Human Events* included *The Greening of America* on its list of the most harmful books of the last two centuries, in a dead heat with Frantz Fanon's *The Wretched of the Earth*.

But Reich's book was a huge popular success, and it took *lifestyle* along with it. There may have been nothing new about the idea that different groups had their own characteristic fashions, morals, and mores. But the moment those patterns started going by the name of *lifestyles*, everybody suddenly had to have one.

That was the moment when marketing analysts were replacing social scientists as new cartographers of the American social landscape. People took to dropping words like *demographics* and *upscale* into their conversations. The old vocabulary of social class was replaced by consumer classifications like *empty nesters*, *Gen X*, *trendies*, and *yuppies*, and the entry requirements for becoming a preppie were relaxed from four years at Andover or Choate to an afternoon at Abercrombie and Fitch.

It wasn't exactly the revolution of consciousness that Reich had had in mind. But the notion of lifestyles flattered people that their consumer choices could be the fundamental fabric of their social identity—or at least for people who had the resources to make them. Not everybody gets to have a lifestyle, after all. You don't see many references to the lifestyles of undocumented immigrants or minimum-wage workers—it's all they can do just to have a life. But for everybody else, lifestyle became the new organizing principle of consumer culture. Treatments for baldness and impotence were rebaptized lifestyle drugs; magazines for skateboarders, gourmets, and travel buffs became lifestyle magazines. The old shopping, fashion, and society pages were merged into a Sunday lifestyle section dedicated to displaying all the rich varieties of having that modern America offers.

And then, there's the vast über-Lifestyle divide between red and blue America, which was first unearthed around the time that Reich's book appeared. In 1970, *Time* magazine named as its man and woman of the year the newly discovered *Middle Americans*, whom it defined by their consumption and leisure habits. Middle Americans, *Time* explained perhaps a little condescendingly, were people who learned baton twirling rather than read Hermann Hesse, who skipped *Midnight Cowboy* in favor of John Wayne in *The Green Berets*, and who preferred the Rockettes at Radio City Music Hall to *Oh! Calcutta!*

There's a direct line from those descriptions down to the picture of an America riven into two nations who are barely capable of speaking to each other, the one listening to Lynyrd Skynyrd in their Chevy Avalanches and the other listening to Radiohead in their Priuses. Contemplating that chasm, commentators have announced with straight faces that the country is more divided than at any time since the Civil War. "You've got 80% to 90% of the country that look at each other as if they were on separate planets," as the Republican strategist Matthew Dowd said not long ago.

Just about everybody seems to accept that view, even if all the data show that the country is actually more uniform in both its culture and its political attitudes than at any time in recent history. As the political scientist Morris Fiorina of Stanford University and the Hoover Institution writes, the two-cultures script "lies somewhere between simple exaggeration and sheer nonsense." But the narcissistic fascination with lifestyles always leads to exaggerating the significance of small differences, which is why the word can be useful to people who want to deny the existence of deep ones.

You can hear that in the way social conservatives denounce the *gay lifestyle* or *homosexual lifestyle*. Gay and lesbian civil rights groups object to those phrases as implying that there's only a single gay lifestyle—the familiar stereotype of poodles, poppers, and promiscuity. But the term is often used as a substitute for homosexuality itself, as in a book title like *Dark Obsession: The Tragedy and Threat of the Homosexual Lifestyle*, the implication being that homosexuality is just another choice like deciding to get a mullet or build a backyard hot tub. That's the underside of our obsession with lifestyles: it makes people seem responsible for everything they are. If you're different from me, you've got nobody but yourself to blame.

LAST PLANET STANDING

Fresh Air Commentary, August 28, 2006

═══════

It isn't completely certain that Mickey Mouse's dog Pluto was named after the planet. As it happens, Pluto was a fairly common name for dogs and horses in the early part of the twentieth century, so the choice of the name for the dog wouldn't have seemed odd in any event. But Disney's bloodhound first appeared under the name Pluto in the cartoon *The Moose Hunt* in 1931, just a year after the announcement that Clyde Tombaugh of the Lowell Observatory in Arizona had discovered a new planet beyond the orbit of Neptune. And it's hard to believe that Disney wouldn't have tried to take advantage of the Plutomania that was sweeping the nation.

After the announcement, thousands of people wrote in to suggest names for the planet. The popular story has it that the name Pluto was submitted by an eleven-year-old British schoolgirl, though the credit for the name most likely belongs to the Italian astronomers who corroborated the discovery photographically.

Meanwhile, Tombaugh himself was lionized as an American hero on the model of Charles Lindbergh—a twenty-two-year-old aw-shucks Kansas farm boy and self-taught astronomer who had beat the best scientists of the rest of the world in the search for the elusive "Planet X" that was thought to be perturbing the orbit of Neptune. And the public's imagination quickened ever more when it was announced, wrongly as it happens, that the new planet was the earth's near twin in mass—as the press put it, it was the only other planet a human being could go to without changing his or her weight.

This had all happened before. William Herschel's discovery of Uranus in 1781 so excited the world that from that moment on, the detection of a new planet epitomized the ecstasy of scientific discovery—the feeling that Keats famously captured in the lines from "On First Looking into Chapman's Homer": "Then felt I like some watcher of the skies / When a new planet swims into his ken." And the discovery of Neptune in 1846 sparked another popular sensation, along with a spirited controversy when the French and English both claimed credit for the first sighting.

But it's not likely any of that will ever happen again. The restrictive definition of a planet that was adopted last Thursday at the meeting of the International Astronomical Union in Prague didn't simply demote Pluto from a planet to what is now called a *dwarf planet*. As several astronomers pointed out, it also made it unlikely that any new objects will be found in the solar system that can qualify for the planet label.

The new definition was chosen over one that would have kept Pluto a planet but would also admit several other bodies to planethood, almost certainly with more in the offing. From

here on in, the number of the planets is necessarily eight—
what the astronomers now refer to as the "classical planets,"
which is just another way of saying a planet that was known
in the day of Jules Verne.

Actually, both the winning and the losing definitions of a
planet had a legalistic feel to them. The astronomers were
clearly less interested in carving nature at the joints than in
finding plausible-sounding criteria that would give due honor
to the cultural significance that people have always accorded to
the notion of a planet. The astronomers implicitly conceded
that the winning definition was ad hoc when they stipulated
that it would only apply to objects in our own solar system,
which is like hearing biologists propose a definition of mam-
mals that only holds for North America. It's a good example of
what legal theorists disparage as result-oriented jurisprudence.
You couldn't help being reminded of the Supreme Court's decision in *Bush v. Gore*, another result-oriented decision that was
"limited to the present circumstances," as the Court put it, and
that couldn't be cited as precedent in other cases.

The interesting question was why it was necessary for the astronomers to go through the whole business in the first place,
and why anybody else should care. After all, language routinely
recognizes natural categories that have no good scientific basis.
There's no compelling geological reason why we should consider Europe a separate continent from Asia, and no botanical
reason why we should refer to tomatoes as vegetables rather
than fruit. There's no way to define the lily that doesn't include
a lot of tulips as well. And other words like *shrub* and *weed* don't
have any kind of scientific definition at all. So why can't we .
just keep using *planet* however we damn well please?

But then the meaning of *planet* has always depended on what science tells us. You can be interested in lilies or tomatoes without caring much about botany. But being interested in planets pretty much guarantees you're an astronomy buff. Since Herschel's day, the idea of other planets has given schoolchildren their first taste of the romance of science—there aren't a whole lot of engineers and physicists who didn't grow up with maps of the solar system on their bedroom walls. It was no doubt in the hope of preserving that romance that the astronomers decided to adopt a definition that closed off the club and expelled Pluto, rather than using one that included Pluto but would also require them to acknowledge a new member every time some astronomer discovered a biggish ice ball in the far reaches of the Kuiper belt.

The irony is that nobody will ever again thrill to the news of a planetary discovery in our solar system. Astronomers will continue to locate curious objects orbiting the sun beyond Neptune, and the discoveries will be given respectful mention on the science pages. But none of those objects is going to have a cartoon character named after it.

THE ROMANTIC SIDE OF FAMILIAR ISSUES

Fresh Air Commentary, September 20, 2006

I have a friend who started his publishing career many years ago in the *New Yorker*'s legendary fact-checking department. After a year or so in the job, he told me at lunch that he had just gotten a promotion: from now on he'd be the fiction checker. "Congratulations," I said, "but what exactly does a fiction checker do?" "Well, there are really two things," he said. "On the one hand, if somebody writes a story about a dentist in Cleveland called Diego Pincowitz, you have to make sure that there actually isn't a dentist in Cleveland by that name. And on the other hand, you want to make sure that nobody gets on a Fifth Avenue bus and goes uptown."

That's how things are supposed to work in fiction—you make up the people and leave the rest of the world as it is. Or if real people do show up under their own names, it's only in cameo appearances, like Napoleon in *War and Peace* or Pauly Shore in an *Entourage* episode. But things get more complicated and controversial when real people move to center stage in the narrative, particularly when they're depicted doing things that never happened, as they were in a 2003 docudrama about Ronald Reagan or the recent ABC docudrama *The Path to 9/11*. What obligation do producers have to get the bus routes right, and to make sure the actual passengers really took them?

Docudramas make literary theorists of us all. In an editorial about the 9/11 miniseries, the *New York Times* drew itself to its full height to lay down the law: "when attempting to re-create real events on screen," it said, "you do not show real people doing things they never did." Meanwhile, defenders of the miniseries were mining literary history to demonstrate that that is exactly what writers have always done. The conservative writer Victor Davis Hanson argued that the script took no liberties that you couldn't find in the works of Bob Woodward, Michael Moore, and Herodotus.

Dramatists have been blending fact and fiction since Aeschylus, and some people like to say it's just docudramas all the way back. True, the term didn't actually enter the language until the 1970s, along with other genre-bending portmanteaux like *infotainment* and *advertorial*. But that hasn't stopped people from using *docudrama* retroactively to refer to Elizabethan political pamphlets or Shakespeare's histories.

Indeed, if there really were nothing more to docudrama than rifling the headlines for dramatic subjects, then the word would apply to movies like *Quiz Show*, *Ali*, *Malcolm X*, or just about every picture Oliver Stone ever made, not to mention old biopics like *The Pride of the Yankees* and *The Glenn Miller Story*—anything, that is, that might describe itself as "based on a true story."

But when most of us talk about docudramas, we're not thinking of movies like *Schindler's List* or *Donnie Brasco*, which borrow from historical sources to create their own dramatic worlds. It isn't likely that J. Edgar Hoover ever actually ate melon from a pool boy's mouth the way Oliver Stone has Bob Hoskins do in *Nixon*. But in the end these movies stand or fall as cinema, not depictions of history, which is why they can be compelling even to people who have no interest in the events they take as their points of departure. People went to see *Raging Bull* because of Martin Scorsese and Robert De Niro, not because they wanted to find out what made Jake LaMotta tick.

But the docudrama was invented as a way of re-creating real events, as the *Times* puts it, and as such it's completely parasitic on them. If you happened to be out of the country when the Elizabeth Smart kidnapping was all over the media, you're not going to be very interested in watching the made-for-TV movie based on it.

Docudramas reshape the events we've been watching on TV according to the well-known rules of TV drama, where stories follow a seven-act trajectory before they're brought to a reassuring moral closure—the object is simply to give us the romantic side of familiar headlines. So the docudrama is by definition a modest form, which avoids drawing any attention to itself as art. The camera angles and lighting are conventional, the scripts are perfunctory and melodramatic, the psychology is simplified to stereotypes that drive the plot, and public figures are played by second-tier actors who are unlikely to leave any strong impression behind them.

Above all, docudramas are eminently forgettable—not just because their believability requires them to be pedestrian, but because they don't have any dramatic existence independent of the stories they re-create. There's nothing older than yesterday's docudrama. Who'd go now to rent any of the docudramas that were made about the Amy Fisher case (there were three of them in all) or the Menendez brothers (two), not to mention *Everybody's Baby: The Rescue of Jessica McClure*? (That was the Jessica who was rescued from the drainpipe in Texas, not the one who was rescued from an Iraqi hospital.)

But for just those reasons, we expect docudramas to be truer than other movies drawn from history. Dramatizing the Reagan presidency or the buildup to 9/11 is not at all the same thing as fictionalizing it, after all. So we take the things that people do and say in docudramas with the same implicit trust that we take the bus routes in a *New Yorker* short story—we assume that everything is as it actually was, only a bit tidier. And when screenwriters misrepresent the events themselves, then the production needs something more than the standard disclaimer about being a dramatization: "What you are about to see is not a dramatization. A lot of this stuff never happened at all."

THE LANGUAGE OF EVE

Fresh Air Commentary, January 3, 2007

====

In 1569, an Antwerp physician and naturalist named Johannes Goropius Becanus published a book arguing that the language spoken in the Garden of Eden must have been Flemish—or more specifically, the Flemish of Antwerp—and that all other languages could be derived from that tongue. According to Becanus, for example, the name Eve came from the Flemish words *eu-vat*—"people barrel" or "barrel of generations"—since all of humanity had its origin in Eve's womb.

Not surprisingly, Becanus's theories were congenial to many of his countrymen, though others found them loopy—Ben Jonson ridiculed him in his play *The Alchemist,* and the philosopher Leibniz turned his name into a verb that means "to speculate foolishly about language." But Becanus's spiritual descendants have flourished over the centuries. Scarcely a day goes by that the group of linguists I post with at the Language Log blog aren't debunking some claim about language that's no less absurd than Becanus's were. So we decided to create the annual Johannes Goropius Becanus award, or Becky for short, awarded to the promulgator of the single most ridiculous or misleading bit of linguistic nonsense that somebody manages to put over in the media.

The year 2006 was rich in contenders. Start with a character named Paul J. J. Payack, who announced last May that using a secret algorithm, he had determined that the English language contained exactly 986,120 words and that it would pass the million mark in the fall. It was a perfect example of what I think of as cow-pie linguistics, but the claim was duly reported by sources like the *New York Times*, Reuters, and NPR.

Then there was the publicist for the British dairy industry who managed to get the BBC to run a story in August that reported with all seriousness that cows from the English West Country moo with a distinct regional accent. If you believe that, I've got a English bulldog who drops his *h*'s I want to sell you. And just last month, the BBC reported that research had shown that British teenagers had become so inarticulate that nearly a third of their speech consists of just twenty simple words like *yeah* and *no*. Actually, that figure is probably about right, but it sounds a lot less alarming when you realize the twenty most frequent English words account for around a third of everybody's speech, whether you're listening to William Safire, Susan Sontag, or the BBC's own news reports.

But by a unanimous vote, this year's Becky goes to the psychiatrist Louann Brizendine, whose best-selling book *The Female Brain* argues that most of the cognitive and social differences between the sexes are due to differences in brain structure. It's a controversial thesis. The *New York Times'* David Brooks and others have hailed the book as a challenge to feminist dogma, and Brizendine herself has charged that her critics are angry because her conclusions aren't politically correct. Actually, though, you can leave out the "politically" part. The reviewers for the British science journal *Nature* described the book as "riddled with scientific errors." And in newspaper commentaries and posts on the Language Log blog, the University of Pennsylvania linguist Mark Liberman has been meticulously debunking Brizendine's claims about men's and women's language.

For example, Brizendine asserts that differences between men's and women's brains make women more talkative than men and goes on to say that women on average use twenty thousand words a day while men use only seven thousand. That factoid comports so neatly with gender stereotypes about chatty women and taciturn men that a lot of people were indignant that anybody would spend money to discover anything so obvious. One reporter at a San Francisco TV station began his story on Brizendine by saying, "Here's a news flash. Women talk more than men. Duh."

Except that—duh!—it isn't true. It turns out that the figures Brizendine reported had been taken from a book by a self-help guru who had simply pulled them out of the air. And the studies that have been done generally show either that men talk slightly more than women or that the two sexes talk about the same amount.

Or take Brizendine's claim that women on average speak twice as fast as men do. That's another cherished bit of gender lore, but no research shows anything of the sort—the best evidence indicates that men on average speak a bit faster than women do. Nor is there any scientific basis for her claims that men think about sex every fifty-three seconds while women think about sex only once a day, or that women are more emotionally attentive because their more sensitive hearing enables them to hear subtle tones and nuances in speech that escape men.

In short, saying that Brizendine's claims about sex differences in language are not exactly scientific gives *not exactly* a bad name. Yet the media generally covered the book uncritically, without running the claims past linguists or neuroscientists or, for the most part, their own science writers, either. In fact the book got much more media attention than any of the serious recent research on the biology of sex differences. That work suggests a more complex picture of the relation between nature and nurture. But in the lifestyle sections where these language items inevitably end up, the preference is for simple stories laced with plausible-sounding nuggets that confirm what we think we already know—that English is the biggest language, that teenagers are inarticulate. Or in this case, that women are congenital chatterboxes. Four hundred and fifty years after Goropius Becanus, we're still easy marks for appealing fables about the language of Eve.

SAY YOU'RE SORRY

Fresh Air Commentary, January 26, 2007

═══

Back in 1971, J. Edgar Hoover gave an interview to *Time* magazine in which he said, "You never have to bother about a president being shot by Puerto Ricans or Mexicans. They don't shoot very straight, but if they come at you with a knife, beware." The remark was widely criticized, and Hoover was obliged to issue a testy explanation. His words had been misinterpreted and taken out of context, he said, adding that he had been privileged to associate with many persons of Puerto Rican and Mexican origin and hadn't intended to cast aspersions on the law-abiding citizens of any ethnic group.

That explanation didn't entirely mollify Hoover's critics, and one Hispanic politician called it a "non-apology." As best I can tell, that was the first time that word had ever appeared in print, and it was another twenty-five years before it became common in the media. The question is, why did it take so long to come up with a word for these things? After all, there's nothing new about nonapologies—public figures over the centuries have always looked for ways to placate the demand for expressions of contrition without having to undergo the self-abasement that sincere apologies entail.

But then no age has ever made such a public spectacle of apologies as ours has. By the time Hoover made his remark, public figures were having to be mindful of heightened ethnic sensitivities and the media's increasing willingness to report the lapses of public figures. And the advent of Nokia, YouTube, and Oprah brought the theater of expiation into its full modern flower. Nowadays every public misstep is apt to be recorded and broadcast, with the offenders obliged to make a round of perp walks on the talk shows, some in an effort to rescue their careers and others in the hope of reviving them.

It isn't a genre that rewards originality, and the performances all follow familiar scripts. Basically, we know everything there is to know about nonapologies by the time we're seven. You make appropriately contrite noises and then go on to point to extenuating circumstances, disclaim any malign intention, and minimize the offense. As in, "Okay, I apologize. But he started it. And I was only kidding. And anyway it was washable ink."

If you're nailed for something you said, you can always claim to have been misinterpreted, the way Hoover did. After the *macaca* episode, Senator George Allen said, "I apologize to anyone who may have been offended by the misinterpretation of my remarks." Or you can express regret over the response to your words, the way Pope Benedict did after his remarks about Islam: "I am deeply sorry for the reactions in some countries to a few passages of my address which were considered offensive."

The same strategy was recently used by Charles Stimson, the Defense Department official in charge of the Guantanamo detainees. In a radio interview, Stimson had said that it was shocking that attorneys from top American law firms were representing accused terrorists, suggested that their corporate clients might want to withdraw their business, and intimated that they might be receiving payments from suspicious sources. After even the administration distanced itself from those remarks, Stimson apologized by saying, "Regrettably, my comments left the impression that I questioned the integrity of those engaged in the zealous defense of detainees." That's like calling somebody an idiot and then saying you're sorry if you left the impression you were impugning his intelligence. But it's a favorite formula for turning a moral transgression into a mere procedural slip-up—not "I said something unacceptable" but "I should have picked my words more carefully, what with how touchy everybody is these days."

Then there are the contingent nonapologies, the ones that come laced with *ifs, anys,* and *may haves.* Mel Gibson reached out to "those who had any heart wounds from something I may have said," as if his anti-Semitic outburst were purely hypothetical. And back in 1992, when Senator Robert Packwood was accused of having sexually assaulted several dozen women, he responded with what has to be the most dubiously penitent nonapology ever offered: "I'm apologizing for the conduct that it was alleged that I did."

It's true that a botched nonapology often compounds an offense by suggesting that the offender is morally clueless in the bargain. But apologies don't always have to be genuine to do their work. In a recent study, the Boston University researchers Richard Ely and Jean Berko Gleason found that the majority of young children's apologies were prompted by adults. It's a fair bet that 95 percent of those prompted apologies were insincere, and the rate is probably equally high for the apologies that public figures are obliged to offer for their transgressions.

But then, does anybody really care whether Pat Robertson was genuinely remorseful about suggesting that Hugo Chavez should be assassinated, or whether Charles Stimson felt a pang of conscience after attacking the lawyers representing the Guantanamo detainees? Sometimes, the more insincere and grudging a nonapology is, the better it makes the point: it doesn't matter whether you're really sorry—if you say this kind of stuff, you're going to have to go out and take it back.

A friend was telling me the other day how she'd made her twelve-year-old son call a girl in his class to apologize for something he'd said. When the girl came on the line, he said, "I'm sorry I called you fat," then hung up the phone. It was pretty clear his apology fell short of true contrition. But my guess is that he learned something anyway.

THE USES OF HYPOCRISY

Fresh Air Commentary, April 17, 2007

═══

What makes the intensity and persistence of the Don Imus flap so curious is that there was no controversy over the remark itself. Left, right, and center, everybody agreed that describing the Rutgers women's basketball team on air as "nappy-headed hos" was beyond the pale of acceptable behavior.

So commentators who were spoiling for an argument were forced to ratchet up the discussion a philosophical notch or two, transforming it into a debate between moral absolutists and moral relativists. For most of the absolutists, the fault was not in condemning Imus, but in the hypocrisy of not condemning others whose offenses were no less reprehensible. Why haven't critics gone after hip-hop lyrics with the same zeal? What about *South Park*, Dave Chapelle, Sarah Silverman, or Borat? Or Al Sharpton? Or Bill O'Reilly? And how can you come down on Imus and give a pass to the anti-Semite T. S. Eliot or the racist D. W. Griffiths?

Then there were the first-amendment absolutists like the *New York Times'* Frank Rich, who deplored the "hypocrisy, sanctimony, and self-congratulation" of Imus's critics, and warned that silencing Imus would have a chilling effect on others who push the line, from Bill Maher and Rosie O'Donnell to Ann Coulter and Glenn Beck. While in the *New York Post,* Kinky Friedman went Rich one—well, make that several—better when he compared Imus to others who were as he lyrically put it, "sacrificed in the name of society's sanctimonious soul," a group in which he included Socrates, Jesus, Galileo, Joan of Arc, Mozart, and Mark Twain.

I can understand some of those concerns. But I also have an intellectual aversion to absolutism. If intelligence consists in being able to make fine distinctions, then it stands to reason that moral absolutism tends to make you stupid. You wind up thinking that the world is really a simple place—or would be, if it weren't for all the excessively clever people who make it more complicated than it is.

So I tend to have more sympathy with the relativists who were trying to sort out all the contextual distinctions that the incident brought into play. Snoop Dogg said that it's one thing when a rapper uses *ho* to refer to some cheap girl in the neighborhood and another when the word is used by an old white man to refer to the Rutgers women's basketball team. In *Time* magazine, James Poniewozik argued that the ironic, self-deprecating Howard Stern could get away with material that sounded offensive in the mouth of the swaggering self-important Imus. And others drew distinctions between ridiculing public and private figures, between talk and drama, or simply between funny and unfunny.

Not all those hairs actually deserved splitting. But it made for a more interesting discussion than the indignant keening of the absolutists. And it doesn't end there. For example, you can be sure that there wouldn't have been much of an uproar over Imus's remark if his show weren't being simulcast over TV, even though a lot more people listen to him on radio than watch him on MSNBC. You think of the way Rush Limbaugh gets away on his radio show with making much more pointed racial cracks than the comparatively benign remark about how the media favor black football players that got him tossed out of his job as an ESPN commentator a couple of years ago. That might be because we think of TV as coming into our homes and of radio as delivered to us when we're alone in our cars, or because we imagine that it's easier to surf inadvertently into a TV program than a radio show. Or maybe it's just that an offensive remark is somehow more disturbing when you see someone making it than when you simply hear him.

But that difference also has to do with the special role we assign to certain TV shows, newspapers, and magazines. It wouldn't bother me to hear Bill Maher describe some politician as a dumb f-word on his HBO show. But it would be rather startling if someone used the same phrase on *Meet the Press*, in a *New York Times* op-ed, or in other forums reserved for our semiofficial discussions of public values. In those spaces, we don't need the FCC to tell us that everyone should be held to a higher standard of propriety. True, the edges of that sanctified region aren't easy to define. What makes the *Times* different from the *New Yorker*, where the f-, a-, and n-words have been nonchalantly appearing for some years now? And Imus's own show falls in a penumbral zone: a radio talk show that was simulcast on a TV news channel, half serious political discussion and half gross-out shock-jockery. It's no wonder people were divided over whether his remark ought to be considered a capital offense, the way it would have been if Brian Williams had made it on the evening news.

To absolutists, that's pure hypocrisy: we permit the offending language in one context while in another we pretend it doesn't exist. On that point, in fact, there's complete agreement between those who want to ban such language everywhere and those who want to remove every restriction on its use.

And it is hypocritical, no question. But then hypocrisy has always gotten a worse rap than it deserves. Back in the seventeenth century, La Rochefoucauld famously described hypocrisy as the homage that vice renders to virtue. But over the long run, homage has a way of turning into genuine respect—as every parent knows, civility has to be forced before it can become sincere. And there's no question we owe a debt to hypocrisy for making us not just a more civil nation, but a more tolerant one. People had to be censured for using the n-word in public before they could begin to understand why it's right to avoid it in private, as well. George Bernard Shaw once observed that hypocrisy is only bad when it is improperly used. It's hard to imagine anything more relativist than that.

THE ENTREPRENEURIAL SPIRIT

Fresh Air Commentary, October 28, 2004

═══════

When the *Oxford Dictionary of Quotations* published its list of the top 101 sayings of 2002, it included a remark that George W. Bush was supposed to have made to Tony Blair: "The problem with the French is that they have no word for 'entrepreneur.'"

After the list appeared, though, a spokesman for the prime minister denied that Bush ever said anything of the sort. I believe him. It sounds like exactly the sort of remark the English would cook up to put in the mouth of an ignorant American.

In fact, despite the right's current disdain for the French and those who speak their language, *entrepreneur* is one of President Bush's favorite words, and he pronounces it with all the sensuous pleasure that foodies give to *mousellines de foie gras*. Speaking in Virginia a few months ago, he said, "entrepreneur—isn't that a lovely word? You know, entrepreneur—we want entrepreneurs."

Entrepreneur first came into English as a fancy name for a theatrical promoter—in French, the word just meant somebody who undertakes something, the same as the Italian *impresario*.

But it was soon being used for people who promoted investments or ran business schemes, occasionally with a slightly unsavory connotation. A 1951 article in the *New York Times* described the gangster Frank Costello as a "slot machine entrepreneur."

The word didn't really come into its own until the Reagan years. As it happens, that was when champions of the free market revived *capitalism* in place of the more genteel-sounding *free enterprise* that had been predominant for most of the century. But the redemption of *capitalism* didn't extend to *capitalist*, which still connoted silk-hatted predators like Henry Clay Frick. *Entrepreneur* seemed ready-made to fill that gap as a name for the risk takers and business builders who were the new heroes of the market economy. An entrepreneur was basically the same thing as a capitalist, only played by Jeff Bridges instead of Lionel Barrymore.

By the 1980s, *entrepreneur* was more than ten times as common in newspaper articles as it had been in the 1950s. Business schools started offering courses in *entrepreneurship*, a word that was practically nonexistent before then. And people retroactively awarded the label to men like Thomas Edison and Henry Ford, who were never called entrepreneurs in their lifetimes. Not to be outdone, management consultants coined the new word *intrapreneur* to describe the plucky self-starters who chose to remain at their corporate jobs—the item gets ten thousand hits on Google.

But in recent years, free-market enthusiasts have been spreading *entrepreneur* around in a new, more democratic way that would have had the French scratching their heads. About a week ago, for example, Commerce Secretary Don Evans complained to Wolf Blitzer that the Democrats have been citing unemployment figures drawn from the payroll survey, rather than the household survey that counts Americans who are self-employed. According to Evans, "Senator Kerry . . . wants to ignore the some 10 million workers in that survey that are the entrepreneurs who are self-employed like truck drivers, like painters, like child-care workers, like hairdressers, like auto mechanics."

Of course for most people *entrepreneur* doesn't bring to mind the guy who does dump runs in his pickup truck or the manicurist who works out of her home. And Evans's description might strike you as just another milestone in the great American tradition of job title inflation. You have the picture of those 10 million entrepreneurs standing shoulder to shoulder with Wal-Mart's 750,000 "sales associates" and the "customer service executives" who answer the phone when you call Comcast to ask about your cable bill.

But the new use of *entrepreneur* is part of a great leveling of the language of modern capitalism, which sweeps away the old distinctions between capital and labor—or at least the growing proportion of the labor force who are foregoing health coverage and a steady salary to make their own way in the world. Last week you were merely an employee; now you're doing the same work on a piecework basis as a paid-up citizen of the ownership society.

Economists have pointed out that the self-employment rate always goes up when the economy heads south. The Economic Policy Institute's Jared Bernstein coined the term *involuntary entrepreneurship* to describe the upsurge—I make that a strong candidate for the American Dialect Society's word of the year. But a lot of people prefer to think of the increase as a healthy flowering of entrepreneurial spirit, after a two-decade decline.

A report from the Kauffman Foundation applauds the sharp rise in self-employment among blacks and Hispanics as a sign that those groups have a higher rate of entrepreneurship than whites and Asians. And the popular conservative blogger Glenn Reynolds sees the shift to the new entrepreneurial economy as presaging decreases in crime and traffic and a more close-knit family life, not to mention a jump in the sale of comfortable office chairs for the home market.

Entrepreneur unquestionably has a lot more cachet than old-economy phrases like *piecework* and *for hire.* But new job titles have a way of losing their luster if they don't come with new carpeting in the bargain. Writers who are paid by the word don't often think of themselves as the medieval knights errant that *freelance* originally brought to mind. For that matter, *employee* doesn't have the panache it did when the Victorians first borrowed it from French as a highfalutin substitute for *clerk.*

So it's unlikely that all those day-care workers and peripatetic car detailers are suddenly going to see themselves as having the same economic interests as Bill Gates and Warren Buffett, even if they all have the same job title on their business cards. What *entrepreneur* really comes down to these days is just "Will undertake for food."

TRUE BRIT

Fresh Air Commentary, July 13, 2005

======

"Brits Maintain a Stiff Upper Lip." That headline in the *Indianapolis Star* last week turns up among more than three hundred stories on Google News that mentioned stiff upper lips to describe the way the British people were reacting to the London bombings, along with hundreds of other stories that used items like *plucky, carrying on,* and *getting on with it.*

Of course the press always finds some characteristic local virtue to extol when attacks like these occur. After 9/11, everybody talked about the way New Yorkers always come together in a crisis. The response to the Madrid bombings last year had the media praising the Spaniards' proud defiance and lust for life—or at least until the Spanish voted in a new government that announced they would be pulling Spanish troops out of Iraq, at which point some commentators on the right started to allude to emotional and volatile Latins. And you can bet that the press would have found other familiar stereotypes to describe the local reaction if the bombings had occurred in Rome or Warsaw or Moline, Illinois.

The fact is that decent people everywhere react to these outrages in pretty much the same way. They feel a swell of anger and fear and sadness and solidarity. And then they show up for work; they get back on the buses and subways; they sit in cafés. When you come down to it, what other choice does anybody have?

Even so, those images of British pluck and fortitude are particularly hard to resist. They have deep roots in the language itself. The phrase *stiff upper lip* was actually an American invention, but it has been associated with a particularly British sort of phlegm since World War I, and it became a cliché during the London blitz. Ira Gershwin wrote a song called "Stiff Upper Lip" for the 1937 musical *A Damsel in Distress*:

> What makes every Englishman
> A fighter through and through?,
> It's just a little thing they sing to one another:
> Stiff upper lip! Stout fella! Carry on, old fluff!

Still, the picture of the British has changed a bit since Ira Gershwin's day. Back then, for example, nobody would have referred to them as "the Brits." That term didn't become popular in America until the 1970s, and it was another decade or two before the British themselves took it up. A friend of mine from London tells of first hearing the word when he arrived in St. Louis to take up a job in 1976. "Are you a Brit?" a store clerk asked him when he heard his accent. My friend was completely mystified. "No," he said. "Actually I'm English."

Of course there are other words that describe the inhabitants of Great Britain as a group. But *Britons* has a musty sound—

you think of "Rule Britannia," not David Bowie or the Buggles. And to Americans, *Britishers* brings to mind droopy moustaches and rolled-up umbrellas. *Brit* is more familiar and affable than those terms—in fact it and *Aussie* are about the only friendly slang words we have for other nationalities. It conjures up a picture of a no-nonsense, unpretentious, middle-class race. *Britishers* are Neville Chamberlain, Margaret Rutherford, and Vita Sackville-West; Brits are Tony Blair, Helen Mirren, and Tina Brown.

It's no accident that *Brit* caught on during the Thatcher years, particularly among journalists and politicians who wanted to portray the UK as our doughty, tough-minded ally, the real spine of the Atlantic Alliance. *Brits* depicts the British as the Europeans you can count on, and a living reproach to the rest of them. It may be that the British populace actually opposes the Iraq war as much as most other Europeans do, but that point tended to get lost in a lot of last week's paeans to British defiance. Unlike the Spaniards, William Bennett said on Fox News, the Brits will step up, the same way they stepped up in World War II—"this is a people that knows how to fight. The British lion will roar."

We pay tribute to that notion of British steel in some of the expressions we've borrowed in recent years. "This is no time to go wobbly, George," Margaret Thatcher famously said to George Bush Sr. during the Gulf War, and the phrase promptly entered the American lexicon as a rebuke of someone who's losing his nerve. "Bush Goes Wobbly on Immigration," read a headline over a *Daily News* editorial a few weeks ago, on the assumption that any New Yorker would catch the allusion.

This all has more to do with us than with them. America and Britain have always adjusted their stereotypes of each other to reflect the vices they most scorn in themselves and the virtues they most admire. The Londoners who are quietly going about their business after the bombings may not be any more plucky or resilient than anybody else would have been in the same circumstances. But they stand in for what we'd like to think is our own better nature.

THE LANGUAGE OF DEATH

Los Angeles Times, February 12, 2007

This week, California Assembly Speaker Fabian Nuñez and a group of Democratic legislators will reintroduce the California Compassionate Choices Act, which would allow terminally ill patients found to be of sound mind to request medication from doctors "to provide comfort with an assurance of peaceful dying if suffering becomes unbearable."

Like the 1994 Oregon Death with Dignity law it is based on, the California bill nowhere mentions suicide, except to say that "actions taken in accordance with this bill shall not constitute suicide or homicide." That clause was framed to address concerns about legal liability and life insurance benefits, but the avoidance of *suicide* is also an implicit acknowledgment of the stigma attached to the s-word. The choice of words makes a big difference in how people come down on laws governing the choice to die. In a 2005 Gallup survey, 75 percent of adults agreed that doctors should be allowed by law to "end the lives" of patients suffering from incurable diseases if the patient and his or her family request it. But when the question was worded as permitting doctors to "assist the patient to commit suicide," only 58 percent of the respondents agreed. That's one reason supporters of the measures have shied away from talking about *assisted suicide* in favor of a battery of gentler phrases, like *aid in dying, choice in dying,* and *end-of-life choices.*

Not surprisingly, opponents hear those phrases as Orwellian euphemisms. When Oregon's Department of Human Services announced that it would be dropping the phrase *assisted suicide* from its Web site, Dr. Charles Bentz, the director of a group opposed to the Oregon law, charged that the department was "trying to take away those stinging, harsh terms that can lead to guilt. They are backing away from calling it what it is— a suicide and an act of medical killing."

But is *suicide* really the appropriate label here? To most of us, the word suggests fanaticism, desperation, or mental unbalance. Certainly most patients who want a doctor's help to end their lives wouldn't qualify as suicidal by the ordinary definition of the term. And like other words ending in the suffix *-cide*, *suicide* has overtones of criminality or wrongdoing—it's an act we speak of people "committing," like grand larceny or adultery. In fact, the *Oxford English Dictionary* defines *suicide* as "the act of taking one's own life" and adds the synonym *self-murder.*

To some of its opponents, *murder* is just what the California bill would permit patients and their doctors to perform. But most people are reluctant to speak of suicide when the choice to die seems defensible or at least understandable, in the same way we don't use *homicide* to describe soldiers who kill in wartime. The New York City medical examiner's office demurred from listing suicide as the cause of death for any of the people who jumped from the World Trade Center on 9/11.

The deaths were recorded as homicides, following the same logic that has the Oregon law instructing doctors to list cause of death as the patient's disease.

Then, too, to describe phrases like *aid in dying* as euphemisms isn't necessarily to condemn them. Every culture and every age has felt the need to find words that palliate the harsh realities of death and dying. Most of the English vocabulary of death had euphemistic origins. *Cemetery* is from the Greek word for a dormitory, and until the Crimean War, *casualty* was just a word for an accidental loss.

Execution and *capital punishment* were introduced to distance the brutal facts of state killing. And *suicide* itself was coined in the seventeenth century as a more decorous name for what Shakespeare called *self-slaughter*. Some euphemisms exist to lessen a sense of culpability—*execution* and *collateral damage*, for example. But most are what the classicist Richmond Lattimore called "the alleviations of death." Terms like *pass away*, *succumb*, *the departed*, and *fallen* serve to comfort the dying and console the living.

Hastened death and *aid in dying* clearly belong in the second group, even if you think they also belong in the first. Or, at least, they're the softened language anyone would choose when sympathizing with a friend whose terminally ill mother had chosen to end her life. When you're speaking to the bereaved, compassion should always trump brutal honesty.

But all of this creates a familiar quandary for the media and government bodies. In an age that has polarized the vocabulary of moral and political values, it can be hard to find neutral linguistic ground. Most media still speak of assisted suicide, whatever reservations people may have about the phrase. For now, anyway, items like *aid in dying* and *end-of-life choices* are simply too vague to convey the specifics of the laws to the average reader. And while a reference in an Associated Press report to "a law that allows doctors to assist in hastening the death of a patient" may be more explicit, it doesn't exactly roll off the tongue.

Ultimately, one or another term may very well emerge from the welter of euphemisms to become the new label for these choices. It's worth remembering that *pro-choice* and *affirmative action* were regarded as oblique euphemisms when they were first introduced, and so were *welfare, social security,* and *free enterprise* in earlier periods.

Even if the media wind up sticking with *assisted suicide*, the terminology controversies are bound to change the way people think about the issue. From civil rights to feminism to gay rights to modern conservatism, the success of influential social movements can be measured by their power to throw our settled vocabulary into disarray.

Separate but equal, ladylike, deviant, liberal, and now *suicide*— when the old words no longer appear transparent and uncomplicated, we're obliged to either abandon them or justify them anew, reexamining our own attitudes along the way.

MARRIAGE KNOT

Fresh Air Commentary, May 28, 2008

A couple of months ago, the editors of the *Oxford English Dictionary* made some long-overdue revisions in the definitions for a bunch of gender-related words. Before then, the dictionary's definition of *girlfriend* in the meaning of "sweetheart" read "a man's favorite female companion," which would have precluded lesbians from having girlfriends in the romantic sense. *Partner* had been defined as "one associated in marriage, a spouse; more frequently applied to the wife." And the old definition of *love* read, "That feeling of attachment which is based upon difference of sex . . . and which is the normal basis of marriage." So the words were all given new definitions that would cover their use to refer to same-sex relationships.

This is hardly a matter of rampant political correctness or of giving the words a new meaning. It isn't as if the English language has ever ruled out talking about lesbians having girlfriends, much less prevented Shakespeare from describing a romantic attachment between two men with the word *love*. It's just that when the definitions were written, those sorts of relationships were officially invisible.

Those redefinitions came to mind as I was listening to the renewed debate about gay marriage. To a lot of people, that notion isn't simply a threat to God's plan or the social order, but an affront to English. In the words of the conservative columnist Paul Greenberg, *gay marriage* is "a desecration of language." Do a Google search for web pages containing *same-sex marriage* and the like together with *oxymoron*, and you turn up over forty thousand hits, most of them posted by people who would tell you that the phrase *same-sex marriage* is as semantically anomalous as *female rooster*.

It isn't likely that many people's reservations about gay marriage spring from their concern for the proprieties of English usage. But it's always useful to be able to frame your position on an issue as a defense of the "traditional definition" of a word. It's a way of folding your argument into the language itself, so that it doesn't require analysis—it makes things as cut and dried as a dictionary entry. Except that the "traditional definition" of a word isn't always that easy to pin down. In retrospect, features that seemed to be part of the essential meaning of a word can turn out to be merely the traces of the social attitudes that used to surround it. Until recently, the OED defined *girl friday* as "a resourceful young woman assistant (to a man)." That says a lot more about how people pictured the office setting than about what the phrase actually meant.

In the case of *marriage*, though, dictionaries themselves aren't necessarily going to be helpful in sorting things out. Lexicographers know that nobody's going to go to the mattresses to defend the traditional definitions of *love* and *girlfriend*. But when it comes to *marriage*, they start looking nervously over both their shoulders. People only look the word up to make a point, and when they don't find what they want, they're liable to organize a letter-writing campaign or punch in an angry blog entry.

Some dictionaries try to placate both sides with a Solomonic solution. Both *Merriam-Webster's* and the *Oxford American Dictionary* have retained their old definition of *marriage* as a union between people of the opposite sex and added an additional definition that applies specifically to same-sex unions that resemble traditional marriages. That recalls the editorial practice the *Washington Times* followed until recently, where it always put "marriage" in quotes when referring to homosexuals.

But there's no way to split the baby here. The opponents of gay marriage won't consent to any official use of the m-word. And its advocates won't accept an asterisk on the word—what point would the whole movement have if *marriage* couldn't have a single meaning that applies to everyone? That's how the word is treated in the Encarta Dictionary, which gives it a single definition that makes no reference to gender: "a legally recognized relationship . . . between two people who intend to live together as sexual and domestic partners."

Like the OED's redefinitions of *love* and *girlfriend*, that's not meant to be a new meaning for the word, but an effort to get at what's really basic to the old one, once you strip away what Edmund Burke called the "ancient prejudices and prescriptions" that traditions are always entangled in.

Of course some people will argue that the definition of *marriage* as a heterosexual union has sacramental roots that make the word very different from *girlfriend* or *love*, while others will respond that marriage has never been an essentially religious notion the way, say, ordination is.

That debate will continue for a long time, or at least until the institution of gay marriage becomes so ordinary and unre-markable that people no longer feel the need to distinguish it with the prefix *gay* in the first place (actually, that's already the way the *New York Times* treats the word in the marriage an-nouncements in its Sunday Styles section). Not that there won't still be people who insist that same-sex couples *shouldn't* be married, but they'll no longer be able to argue that they logi-cally *couldn't* be.

In the meantime, though, the discussion would benefit if everybody could agree to lose the word *traditional*, which has probably worked as much mischief over the last half century as any other word in American public life. It's a word people use to muddle the past, so it doesn't have to explain or justify itself. In fact when people defend something as traditional, what they have in mind almost always turns out to be a purely modern concoction, like the pastiche of Chippendale, French provincial, Queen Anne, and colonial that goes by the name of "traditional" on an Ethan Allen bedroom set. *Traditional mar-riage* brings to mind the same sort of thing: a hodgepodge of customs, laws, and restrictions, secular and religious, jumbling places and periods willy-nilly. In either case, you can't tell what's the frame and what's the filigree.

HONOR BE TO MUDJEKEEWIS!

Language Log, June 26, 2006

═══════

In my in-box, every morning,
Scads of spam solicitations,
Each, to fool the filters, strewing
In the header and the body,
Random lines from "Hiawatha":
"And Nokomis warned her often"
Get your clearitol and cum pills;
"O beware of Mudjekeewis"
Make your wife or girlfriend speechless;
"Lie not down upon the meadow"
Safe Prescription Medication;
"And Nokomis fell affrighted"
Over half a million clients;
"Downward through the evening twilight"
Free Fed-Ex on every order;
Till I have the sense of hearing
The entire fucking cosmos

Droning, unenjambed, insistent,
In tetrameter trochaics,
Lulling me to drowsy numbness . . .
"Wahonowin! Wahonowin!"
May already be a winner!

WORD INDEX

SUBJECT INDEX

See also Conservatives;
  Neoconservatives
"Road Not Taken, The," 6
Robertson, Pat, 174, 220
Robeson, Paul, 14
Robson, Catherine, 6
Rock, Chris, 26
Rockefeller, Nelson, 61
Rockwell, Norman, 94
Rogers, Will, 62
Roosevelt, Franklin D., 76, 91, 166, 168
Rothschild, Lady Lynn Forester de, xvi–xvii
Rove, Karl, 11, 40, 98, 163
Rubin, Jerry, 26
Rubin, Robert, 199
Rumsfeld, Donald, 48
Russell, Alec, 169
Rutherford, Margaret, 231

Sackville-West, Vita, 231
Safire, William, 34, 60, 107, 109, 184, 214
St. Valentine's Day, 142
Salon.com, 117
Same-sex relationships, 237. *See also* Homosexuality
San Diego Union-Tribune, 174
San Francisco Chronicle, 117
Santorum, Rick, 81–82
Sarcasm, 28, 29, 30, 39
SAT essays/exams, 152, 182
Satire, 73
Savonarola, 82
Scalia, Antonin, 69
Schiavo, Terri, x

Schiller, Friedrich, 170
Schindler's List (movie), 210–211
Schütze, Hinrich, 138
Schwarzenegger, Arnold, 60, 62, 79
"Scots wha' hae' wi' Wallace bled," 6
Scott, Hugh 60n
Search engines, 129, 131, 132, 138. *See also* Google
Semantics, xi, xii
Sexuality, 27, 131, 143, 159, 202, 215–216, 219, 239
  sexual revolution, 26
  sexual slurs, 9
  See also Homosexuality
Shakespeare, William, 235, 237
Sharpton, Al, 221
Shaw, George Bernard, 224
Shils, Edward, 180
Show Boat (musical), 14
Shue, Henry, 51
Silverman, Sarah, 221
Sinatra, Frank, 14n
Sirota, David, 76
Sitcoms, 74, 75
Skinner, David, 202
Skippy the Bush Kangaroo blog, 117
Slang, 151, 191, 231
Slashdot (Web site), 126, 127
Slate, 117
Sloan, Alfred P., 91
Slogans, xiv, xv
Slurs, 9, 83
Smut, 74, 75
Snoop Dogg, 222
Snow, Tony, xii, 86

PEG SKORPINSKI

GEOFFREY NUNBERG is a linguist who teaches at the School of Information of the University of California at Berkeley and is the chairman emeritus of the Usage Panel of the American Heritage Dictionary. His commentaries on language and politics have appeared regularly on NPR's *Fresh Air* and in the Sunday *New York Times* and many other publications and have earned him the Linguistic Society of America's Language and the Public Interest Award. His books include *Going Nucular*, *Talking Right*, and *The Way We Talk Now*. Nunberg lives in San Francisco, California.

PublicAffairs is a publishing house founded in 1997. It is a tribute to the standards, values, and flair of three persons who have served as mentors to countless reporters, writers, editors, and book people of all kinds, including me.

I. F. STONE, proprietor of *I. F. Stone's Weekly*, combined a commitment to the First Amendment with entrepreneurial zeal and reporting skill and became one of the great independent journalists in American history. At the age of eighty, Izzy published *The Trial of Socrates*, which was a national bestseller. He wrote the book after he taught himself ancient Greek.

BENJAMIN C. BRADLEE was for nearly thirty years the charismatic editorial leader of *The Washington Post*. It was Ben who gave the *Post* the range and courage to pursue such historic issues as Watergate. He supported his reporters with a tenacity that made them fearless and it is no accident that so many became authors of influential, best-selling books.

ROBERT L. BERNSTEIN, the chief executive of Random House for more than a quarter century, guided one of the nation's premier publishing houses. Bob was personally responsible for many books of political dissent and argument that challenged tyranny around the globe. He is also the founder and longtime chair of Human Rights Watch, one of the most respected human rights organizations in the world.

·   ·   ·

For fifty years, the banner of Public Affairs Press was carried by its owner Morris B. Schnapper, who published Gandhi, Nasser, Toynbee, Truman, and about 1,500 other authors. In 1983, Schnapper was described by *The Washington Post* as "a redoubtable gadfly." His legacy will endure in the books to come.

Peter Osnos, *Founder and Editor-at-Large*